Problem-solving in Organizations

This concise introduction to the methodology of business problem-solving (BPS) is an indispensable guide to the design and execution of practical projects in real organizational settings. The methodology is both result-oriented and theory-based, encouraging students to use the knowledge gained on their disciplinary courses, and showing them how to do so in a fuzzy, ambiguous and politically charged, real-life business context. The book provides an in-depth discussion of the various steps in the process of business problem-solving. Rather than presenting the methodology as a recipe to be followed, the authors demonstrate how to adapt the approach to specific situations and to be flexible in scheduling the work at various steps in the process. It will be indispensable to MBA students who are undertaking their own fieldwork.

Dr Joan Ernst van Aken is Professor of Organization Science at the Department of Organization Science and Marketing of the Faculty Technology Management, Eindhoven University of Technology, The Netherlands.

Dr Hans Berends is Assistant Professor in the Department of Organization Science and Marketing of the Faculty Technology Management, Eindhoven University of Technology, The Netherlands.

Dr Hans van der Bij is Assistant Professor in the Department of Organization Science and Marketing of the Faculty Technology Management, Eindhoven University of Technology, The Netherlands.

Problem-solving in Organizations

A Methodological Handbook for Business Students

Joan Ernst van Aken
Hans Berends
Hans van der Bij

CAMBRIDGE UNIVERSITY PRESS
Cambridge, New York, Melbourne, Madrid, Cape Town, Singapore, São Paulo

Cambridge University Press
The Edinburgh Building, Cambridge CB2 2RU, UK

Published in the United States of America by Cambridge University Press, New York

www.cambridge.org
Information on this title: www.cambridge.org/9780521869768

First published 2007

Printed in the United Kingdom at the University Press, Cambridge

A catalogue record for this book is available from the British Library

ISBN-13   978-0-521-86976-8 hardback
ISBN-10   0-521-86976-5 hardback

Contents

Part III On methods 127

Part IV   Conclusion   **169**

Figures

Boxes

Preface

This handbook gives the methodology for problem-solving in organizations or, in other words, for business problem-solving. Its target audience consists of graduate business students aiming to develop their competences in business problem-solving, not just on the basis of written cases but in a real-life context. Junior management consultants or researchers involved in problem-solving within the framework of Action Research may also find the methodology of this handbook useful.

The theory in this handbook can best be mastered through an extensive classroom course, although it may be possible to study the material in a more accelerated version for those able to back it up with self-study and fieldwork. As well as addressing the theories, training should be provided on issues such as problem definition, developing a project proposal, problem analysis, and solution design. Ideally, training in the classroom should be followed by further development of competences by actual problem-solving in the field.

Since its scientification, the field of business and management has developed into a respectable social science. This has led to the idea that the core competence of the business graduate is undertaking good research and that fieldwork for a business student should reflect this. However, we feel that the core competence of the business graduate is business problem-solving. Business problem-solving is very different from business research. There are many books on business research methodology, which is quite similar to more general social science research methodology. They give the methodology for analysing, describing and explaining *that what is*, focusing on the development of (usually general) knowledge. In business problem-solving, on the other hand, the focus is on designing *that what can be*, or *that what should be* in order to improve the performance of a specific business system on one or more criteria. In order to be able to design a business system, or to redesign an existing one, one must analyze the present one and the possible causes of its less than satisfactory performance. For that, many classic (and non-classic for that matter) methods of social science research can help. But problem analysis is only the first part of business problem-solving, and analysis should be in the service of the design of solutions (and the necessary change plans). Therefore the methodology given here is *design-focused*: problem-solving projects aim at the design of a sound solution and at the realization of performance improvement through planned change, and not merely at sophisticated analyses or smart reports.

The methodology of this handbook is also *theory-based*. In practice, problem-solving in organizations is often undertaken in a craftsman-like fashion, based on business experience and informed common sense. The methodology presented in this book is theory-based: based on state-of-the-art literature, on the type of business systems and type of problems in question, and on the methods to be used in solving business problems (without, of course, discounting off common sense and experience).

Our approach builds on the traditions of rational problem-solving. The type of problems best suited to this approach should have a significant technical-economic content. At the same time we recognize that organizations are social systems, that the realization of improvements in business system performance entails organizational change, and that effective organizational change does not only need technical-economic interventions (like the presentation of a promising solution for a problem), but political and cultural ones as well. Therefore our focus is not only on technical solution design, but also on the design of the change process needed to realize the performance improvement, and on the development of organizational support for a solution and change plan.

The prime objective of problem-solving projects for students is to develop their core competence, that is their competence in business problem-solving. These projects should, of course, also serve the interests of client organizations by supporting their problem-solving. For university or college supervisors, student problem-solving projects can also provide valuable input to their research. The problem in question will normally be within the scope of their sub-discipline in business, and they can use their business contacts to find organizations with problems within their specific research area. Student problem-solving projects can then provide supervisors with useful additional insight into current business issues and often also some empirical data.

Field problem-solving can be a very important element in a business course programme as it aims to develop the core competence of the student. But it is done in a terrain with more pitfalls and booby traps than a university library. We hope that the methodology given in this handbook will help the student to navigate this difficult but important and interesting terrain.

Joan Ernst van Aken
Hans Berends
Hans van der Bij
Eindhoven, January 2006

Part I

Fundamentals

In Part I we discuss the general background of problem-solving in organizations. We start by describing the characteristics and general setup of problem-solving projects, which aim to improve the performance of a certain business system on one or more performance indicators in the real world. We compare this with business research projects, which aim to develop general knowledge. We then discuss the characteristics of the methodology for business problem-solving presented in this handbook, and compare this with other problem-solving strategies. As design is a key activity in our approach, we provide some general design theory plus some theory on social system design. Finally, we discuss the various sources of knowledge to be used in business problem-solving, and the development of general design knowledge through scholarly research.

1   Scope and nature of this handbook

1.1 Objectives and target audience

This handbook gives a design-focused and theory-based methodology for business problem-solving projects, be they large or small, driven by one or a group of business students in consulting roles. Our methodology has been developed for university business programmes such as MBA programmes, for which the development of student competences to solve real-life business problems is a key objective. Or, in other words, for business courses that aim to educate professionals. The core competence of the scientist is research, but for professionals such as doctors, lawyers and engineers, it is problem-solving in the field. For the business student the development of that competence can be supported by in-house courses on problem-solving methodology and courses based around written case-studies, but in our opinion its key component should be business problem-solving (BPS) in a real-life context. This can be achieved either by a trainee within a company taking on a BPS project of six months or so, or as a smaller project undertaken by a group of students visiting a company on a few occasions to do their analysis and present their proposals.

This handbook can be used in a general classroom course to prepare for business problem-solving fieldwork, and subsequently as a sourcebook for preparing and running actual field projects. It can also be used as additional reading (possibly with one or more classroom training sessions) for a disciplinary course aiming to combine theory with the application of that theory in practice.

The methodology of this handbook has been developed based on more than ten years' experience in supervising business problem-solving projects by students of the techno-MBA course at Eindhoven University of Technology. These included short group assignments in BPS in the field, but most were six- to nine-month graduation projects, aimed at further developing students' competences in theory-based BPS. The business problems to be solved typically had a significant technical-economic content. However, this handbook deals with the conceptual and technical setup of the project itself, not with methods related to the content of the problem. Unlike many books on consulting (see for example Albert 1980; Kubr 1996), this book does not have sections on problem-solving in different disciplinary contexts. Typically in the context of a university course, university supervisors will provide students with the necessary disciplinary support. Chapter 3 provides further discussion on the nature and application of our methodology for business problem-solving.

1.2 Design-focused and theory-based business problem-solving

As will be discussed in more detail in Chapter 2, a BPS project typically consists of an analysis and design part, an organizational change part, and a learning part, during which the organization learns to realize improved performance on the basis of the designed solution. The methodology presented in this handbook focuses on the design of the solution for the business problem, the design of the change process needed to realize that solution in new or adapted roles and procedures, and the analyzes needed to make those designs. Hence the term 'design-focused'. We will only briefly discuss the change and learning part, reflecting the actual practice of business students undertaking a business problem-solving project. Typically they will focus on the two designs (and work on organizational support for these designs), but will leave the – possibly quite protracted – change and learning parts to the organization itself. Therefore our focus is largely on the design part of the BPS project.

'Theory-based' means that in this approach problem-solving is not done in a craftsman-like way, largely relying on one's own experience and informed common sense. Rather, it is theory-based, using state-of-the-art literature. The literature to be used in business problem-solving entails two complementary aspects:

– *object* and *realization knowledge*: knowledge of the *object* of problem-solving, that is, knowledge of organizations and management in general, and of various business systems and functions such as marketing, operations, innovation and finance in particular; and knowledge of the *realization* of business solutions through planned change;
– *process knowledge*: that is, knowledge of approaches and methods to be used in the analysis and design of business solutions and change plans, from

problem definition to decision-making on proposed solutions and change plans.

This handbook focuses on the second category, that of process knowledge for business problem-solving. It also discusses some elements of realization knowledge in the context of change plan design, but it does not discuss object knowledge as this will be provided by the disciplinary courses of the business programme, supported by the university supervisors of the BPS project.

'Theory-based' does not, of course, mean copying theory into particular cases. Theory is by definition general and must always be contextualized for use in actual problem-solving. Theory-based in BPS within an academic programme specifically means the *comprehensive, critical and creative use of theory*:

– *comprehensive*: because problem-solving should be based on a systematic review of the existing literature on the issues in question;
– *critical*: because one should judge the value and limitations of existing literature, among other things on the basis of the evidence given (for instance the design of business solutions may be informed by management literature, as long as one is aware of its limitations);
– *creative*: because one should not just use theory, but aim to build upon it, play with it, and add to it in order to produce appealing designs.

Theory-based design can be seen as design on an academic level, in which theory is very important, but at the same time with an awareness of its limitations.

1.3 How to use this handbook

This handbook provides theory on how to set up and drive a BPS project. It should be used in a comprehensive, critical and creative way. By comprehensive we mean that the theory should not be used as a menu by which readers pick and choose certain elements. Rather the approach as a whole should be followed. At the same time the theory should be used critically, as far as is appropriate for the business problem in question. Chapter 3 supports the critical use by discussing the limitations of this theory and the types of problems for which it can be used. The creative use means that the approach given in this book is not simply to be copied, but that it is to be contextualized. The approach given in this handbook should be regarded as a 'design model'; a general model to be used as the basis for the design of the specific setup of a BPS project for a specific setting. The approach of this handbook is a kind of 'norm process'; a well-tested example of how to do it, described in terms of a 'standard setting'. In reality no setting is standard, so one always has to make one's own, specific project design. At the same time one should be able to justify any deviation from the norm process on the grounds of the requirements of the specific setting, or on the grounds of the recognized limitations of the norm process itself.

Although in our experience graduate students are quite able to use a handbook such as this in self-study, to prepare and manage their BPS projects in the field, a good way to learn this approach is to follow a classroom course using this book. We use it in a course consisting of a few explanatory lectures, self-study, and a number of training sessions in which written case studies are used to train for activities such as problem definition, designing a problem-solving approach, and preparing a project proposal. However the real learning experience should be in the field: defining problems, capturing data and exploring solutions in the messy, political and sensitive world of real-life business, thus developing the tacit knowledge needed to apply the codified knowledge of the business programme. No written case study can give the student that learning experience. Even students with previous business experience, who tend to tackle problems on the basis of their experience and common sense, can benefit from this theory-based, design-based approach to business problem-solving.

2   Problem-solving projects in organizations

2.1   The nature of business problem-solving projects

The objective of this handbook is to discuss the methodology of business-problem solving (BPS) projects, carried out by business students. Examples of such projects are:

- improving the delivery performance of the spare part inventory control of a capital goods company;
- developing a cost control system for a distribution centre of a postal service;
- improving the performance of a recently introduced e-procurement system for a small company;
- developing a decision support system for the allocation of resources to research and design projects for a small, high-tech company;
- developing a system for measuring the performance of a marketing and sales department;
- improving the effectiveness and efficiency of training courses for the human resources management department of a large company;
- developing a system for measuring the reliability of new software in a software development department;
- improving the quality control system of a production department by introducing statistical process control.

Business problem-solving projects are started to improve the *performance* of a business system, department or a company on one or more criteria. Ultimately it should impact the profit of a company (or a comparable overall performance indicator if it is a not-for-profit-organization), but usually the actual objectives of a BPS project are of a more operational nature, related to the effectiveness and/or efficiency of operational business processes. The approaches discussed in this handbook can generally also be used for business improvement projects of a more strategic nature, although we do not discuss the additional technical-economic, political and social complexities of such projects here.

BPS projects are undertaken to improve the performance of a certain business system or organizational unit. With respect to the logic of their setup we will follow the classic problem-solving cycle as elaborated in the *regulative cycle* by Van Strien (1997). This regulative cycle has five basic process steps (see figure 2.1 below):
- problem definition;
- analysis and diagnosis;
- plan of action;
- intervention;
- evaluation.

This is the logic of the regulative cycle from the perspective of the student. From the perspective of the client organization a full BPS project has three parts:
- a *design part*, in which a redesign of the business system or organizational unit is made based on the problem definition, analysis and diagnosis; a change plan for introducing the redesign; and the development of an organizational support structure for the solution and change plan (steps 1, 2 and 3 of the regulative cycle);
- a *change part*, in which the redesign is realized through changes in organizational roles and routines, plus the possible implementation of new tools or information systems (step 4 of the regulative cycle);
- a *learning part*, in which the client organization learns to operate within the new system and with the new instruments, and learns to realize the intended performance improvement. An organization needs time to recover after a significant change. People have to relearn how to work effectively and efficiently within their new situation, which takes time, effort and management attention. Of course, if the change has been limited, the recovery period can also be limited. (This part of the process may be subsumed under step 5 of Van Strien's regulative cycle.)

Usually the student leaves the company after the design part, having created as far as possible the conditions for a successful outcome of the two subsequent parts. Thus the focus of this handbook is on the design part of the BPS project.

A problem can be defined as the result of a certain perception of a state of affairs in the real world with which one or more important stakeholders are dissatisfied. Business problems have a number of characteristics, many of them very different from research problems. These include the following:

- business problems are not given, cannot be 'discovered' in reality, but are the result of *choices* of influential stakeholders: in the context of a 'mess' of issues, of opinions and value judgments on those issues, of interests, power and influence, these stakeholders choose an issue, or combination of issues, to work on (see Ackoff 1981a, on the problem mess);
- these influential stakeholders are dissatisfied on the basis of a comparison of their *perception of the performance* of the business system in question on certain implicit or explicit *performance indicators* with some implicit or explicit *norms*, and they choose the problem to work on because they have the impression that significant performance improvement is feasible within acceptable constraints on time and effort;
- business problems, like all design problems, are open-ended: typically there is not one unique solution to a business problem, but there can be several good solutions;
- they are not intellectual questions, but are charged with values, interests and power, that is, they are strongly dependent on value judgments of various stakeholders and they are connected with material and immaterial interests of these stakeholders, who may use their formal and informal organizational power to protect those interests;
- typically business problems are solved within (often tight) constraints of time and effort, so analysis and design are done on a satisficing basis, in other words on a 'good enough' basis (even in high-quality, theory-based business problem-solving);
- business problems are selected from a 'problem mess' and subsequently 'solved' through a 'change muddle'. Even if based on a sound solution design and a sound change plan, the actual change and subsequent learning processes are subject to all kinds of external and internal interferences, so that corrective actions and improvisations still play an important role during these change and learning processes, hence the term 'change muddle'.

An important part of problem definition during the course of a BPS project is to make explicit the perceptions, performance indicators and norms used by the various stakeholders in defining their own version of the problem. The problem definition should lead to a definition of a *real problem*. One should avoid doing a BPS project on a *perception problem*; a problem defined on the basis of inaccurate perceptions of the performance of the business system in question. One should also not take on a project on a *target problem*, that is a problem defined on the basis of unattainable norms.

Most business problems are solved by responsible management and/or by the organizational members affected by the problem. However, this handbook

takes the perspective of a business student – an involved outsider to the organizational setting in question – whose help is enlisted to solve the problem
in a consulting role. Graduate business students are people with the expertise
and drive to analyze the problem, design a solution, design a change process
(usually in cooperation with people from the business system in question), and
mobilize organizational support for the solution and change plan. However
they do not have the authority and power to commit organizational resources
or to change the business system, in which case they would also have responsibility for its performance. So they have an *effort commitment*, but not a *result
commitment*.

Because of the characteristics of business problems, discussed above, a BPS
project driven by one or more business students has a number of properties,
including the following:
- the project is not based on an agreement to perform an agreed activity, but
  an agreement to help solve a well-defined business problem;
- definition of the problem is an essential part of the project; the student is
  not someone who simply does what has been asked, but a partner in the
  problem-solving process;
- the problem is demarcated in a such a way that it is large enough for its
  solution to have a significant impact on the performance of the business
  system in question, but small enough for its solution to be feasible in view
  of the time and effort committed by the client organization and the student
  themselves;
- the objective of the project is the realization of an actual performance
  improvement, not the report describing the solution and its implementation, nor the solution itself;
- the student has an *effort commitment*, not a *result commitment*, because,
  as an involved outsider, he/she does not have the authority to commit and
  manage the resources needed to implement the solution and to secure its
  outcomes.

A student BPS project should be interesting enough for the client organization
to invest in it time and management attention (and funds), for the student
to have an important learning experience, and ideally for supervisors to gain
additional insight in current field issues in their research domain. Nevertheless,
normally a student BPS project has a fairly limited scope, although, sometimes
students are asked to address problems that are quite important for the client
organization. Student BPS projects are generally low-profile projects for the
client organization, and management may therefore prefer to ask a student,
rather than a well-known consultancy firm, to address a problem that might be

sensitive. Typically a student's arrival in a firm is not experienced as disruptive by the organization as is that of a consultancy firm, and interviews by students may more easily get the real story from people than interviews by senior consultants. Therefore, student assignments can address problems that are of importance for the organization.

A business problem-solving project involves the analysis of the problem and its context. This analysis is not an end in itself, but 'analysis for design': made to support the solution design. So all kinds of decisions on the scope, level of detail and perspectives to be used in the analysis are to be based on a need-to-know-for-design. Often this makes it necessary to explore some possible solution concepts early on in the analysis, after which the analysis is continued to enable the choice of solution concept and to prepare the subsequent detailed design of the solution.

The designed solution is also not an end in itself, but a means to improve performance: the whole project is focused on performance improvement and not on the beauty or intellectual appeal of the design. A full BPS project entails the analysis of the problem and its context, the design of a sound solution for that problem, the actual change of organizational structures and/or work processes, and the subsequent management of the new situation, in order to produce the intended performance improvement.

In the course of a BPS project the student generally produces three designs:
- a *project plan*: the design of the process that is to produce the solution design and the change plan design, the actions to take and the actors involved (not only the student but also various others who may be involved in analysis and design), and the design of the approach to the analysis and diagnosis of the problem;
- a *solution (or object) design*: the design of the solution of the problem, for example in the form of a new organizational structure, a new work process or a new business information system;
- a *change plan (or change process design)*: the design of the process that is to realize the object design (in terms of the actions to be taken and the actors involved).

The client organization may generally expect the following deliverables:
- a problem definition;
- a problem analysis and a diagnosis of the major causes and consequences of the problem;
- an exploration of potential solutions for the problem;
- an elaboration of one of them in a detailed solution design and a change plan;

– a more intangible deliverable relating to organizational support for the solution and change plan.

The last two deliverables are the key ones, intended to drive – after the student has left the company – the subsequent change and learning processes. The other deliverables are not only to enable the solution design and change plan; they are in themselves of value to the client company. The change and learning processes have been characterized above as a 'change muddle', because of the many outside and inside interferences these processes typically are subjected to and because of the adaptations and improvizations these interferences may necessitate. When things do not develop as designed, as is often the case, it is useful to return to the original problem, its analysis and diagnosis, and the alternative solutions, to see how the designs can be adapted to the new situation, even if the adaptation is only a minor one.

Finally, one may remark that a BPS project is fundamentally different from a research project, as is the subject of books on business research or business research methodology, such as Brewerton and Millward (2001) and Jankowicz (2004). The objective of a research project is to develop knowledge. In an academic context that is general knowledge; in a business context it is specific knowledge, like the motivation of one's employees or the preferences of one's customers. The purpose of research is to solve a *knowledge problem* in the immaterial world of knowledge. The purpose of a BPS project, on the other hand, is to solve a business *performance problem* in the material world of action; it is aimed at actual change and improvement in this material world. In order to achieve this one needs knowledge – the analysis and diagnosis part of the project – but everything is done with the eventual performance improvement in mind. A series of BPS projects followed by reflection and cross-case analyses may be used to develop general business design knowledge, but that is not the subject of this handbook. Ever since the publication of Herbert Simon's classical book *The Sciences of the Artificial* (Simon 1996; original edition 1969) we are aware of the fundamental differences between describing that what is and designing that what can be. This book is interested in that second category of endeavours.

2.2 The basic setup of a problem-solving project

The BPS project follows the logic of the problem-solving cycle, here in the version of the regulative cycle. Figure 2.1 gives the basic process of this regulative cycle.

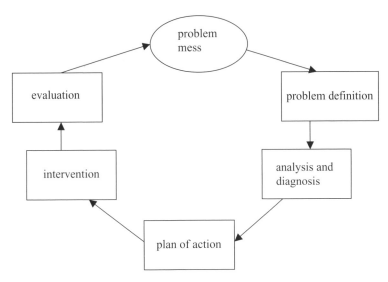

Figure 2.1   The regulative cycle (Van Strien 1997)

The *problem definition* step drives the whole BPS project. It is based on an agreement between the principal of the project and the student (plus the university supervisors). Defining the problem starts with the problem as stated by the principal, but the problem eventually agreed is not necessarily equal to this initial statement. Of course the student should respect this initial problem statement, but problem analysis may show that the initial problem is a perception problem or a target problem, or may show that the problem is only a symptom of an underlying problem and that it cannot be solved without solving that underlying one. So the initial problem statement has to be put in the context of the 'problem mess, followed by a thorough scoping process. The problem should be large enough that its solution contributes significantly to performance and small enough to be solved within the prevailing constraints in time and effort.

Finally, the problem definition is not always static. On the basis of further analysis and design the problem may prove to be more difficult to solve than anticipated, so it may be advisable to scope it down. Alternatively, if the project shows that there is more potential for improvement than anticipated, so one might want to enlarge the scope of the problem. In either case, possible changes in the problem definition should always be well-managed and agreed with the principal.

During the *problem definition* step one also designs the project plan and one's approach to the subsequent analysis, diagnosis and design (see Chapter 5).

The *analysis and diagnosis* step is the analytical part of the project. For this step most of the traditional methods of business research – be they quantitative or qualitative – can be used. Object knowledge with respect to the type of business system and the type of problem should be used to interpret the results of the analysis and to support the diagnosis of the causes of the problem. This analysis and diagnosis step produces specific knowledge on the context and nature of the problem. As we will see, for this *specific* understanding quality criteria like validity and reliability can be applied, which are quite similar to the quality criteria for *general* knowledge resulting from descriptive business research.

During the *plan of action* step one designs the solution for the problem and the associated change plan. For this one can use valid knowledge from descriptive research. The most powerful support, however, can be given by field-tested and grounded technological rules or solution concepts, developed by business research on the basis of the principles of design science research (see Chapter 4.3). Ideally a systematic review of the literature should result in a range of solution concepts to solve the business problem. Out of this range an appropriate one is chosen, whereupon a specific variant of it is designed, adapted to the specific problem and its context in question. Design science research in business is not yet very common, but with sufficient creativity a student is usually quite able to design satisfactory solutions on the basis of descriptive research and local business experience.

If the solution to a business problem involves the redesign (and implementation) of a work process or organizational structure, this redesign from the general to the specific by the student is followed by a second redesign. As will be discussed in more detail in Chapter 3.6 this is the redesign by the members of the organization of their own activities on the basis of the design made by the student. The latter design almost always only specifies the formal system; the organizational actors themselves fill in all the details of the informal system which enables the redesigned work process to perform properly and effectively.

During the *intervention* step roles and work processes are changed on the basis of the solution design and change plan. Usually the student has left the company by then. As discussed above, the next step is the process of learning to work within the new system and to realize the intended performance improvement – a process needing time, effort and management attention. Therefore it is good to plan a formal *evaluation* at a point in time, when one expects most of the learning to have been achieved, to see what still has to be done to realize the full potential of the new system.

2.3 Quality criteria for problem-solving projects

A sound BPS project has to satisfy the following quality criteria:
— performance-focused;
— design-oriented;
— theory-based;
— justified;
— client-centred.

Performance-focused means that the actual performance improvement is the primary objective of the project and that analysis and design are 'just' means to that end. The BPS project is not a purely intellectual exercise but a real-world activity. It is not the beauty of the analysis or the sophistication of the solution that counts (however desirable these may be), but the potential for performance improvement created by the analysis and design for the company in question.

Design-oriented means that the activities during the project are controlled through a sound project plan, as opposed to improvisation. This is not to say that the project plan is a fixed contract to be fulfilled, but that one follows the principle 'look before you leap'. The project plan written during the early stages of a project may give only an outline of the actions to be taken, to be detailed later on, and adapted to incorporate new insights as the project progresses.

Design-oriented also means, of course, that much effort is put into the design of the solution (the object design) and into the accompanying change process, as opposed to solving the problem through improvisation.

Theory-based means that one uses valid, state-of-the-art knowledge for the analysis and design activities and that one is aware of the quality of the knowledge to be used (see Chapter 12). Re-inventing the wheel is not professional, and neither is designing solutions for transport problems without wheels if wheels would do the job best. This knowledge concerns object, realization- and process knowledge. As said in Chapter 1.2, this also means the comprehensive, critical and creative use of theory.

With respect to *object knowledge*: knowledge of the problem and its possible solutions, deciding which categories of literature to use can be a challenge, as can finding the appropriate search terms to use in one's literature search. In Chapter 5.5 we discuss the 'naming and framing' of the problem. The 'naming' of the problem largely defines the kind of solution concepts to use in solution design, but other types of literature may shed further light onto the problem. The choice of literature is reflected in the conceptual project design (see Chapter 5).

With respect to *realization knowledge*: knowledge with respect to managed change processes, the literature search is less complex. There are various types of change processes, but usually the general literature on managed or planned change is fairly easily translated for use in one's own, specific change process. As opposed to some (scholarly) object knowledge, much of it is sufficiently design-oriented to support the design of a managed change process.

Process knowledge is knowledge that can be used to design the analysis and design process. There is a huge amount of literature on analysis of business systems and situations. However, there is much less literature on the design of the overall approach to a BPS project and on the design of solutions for business problems. This handbook is an attempt to redress the balance.

Finally, a theory-based approach to business problem-solving also means that one is critical in the use of literature. Chapter 12 discusses quality criteria with respect to the general theory and with respect to context-specific knowledge to be used in solution design. Management literature written by managers or consultants for managers or consultants often does not meet these criteria. There is also scholarly literature that can be criticised on the basis of these criteria. This does not mean that such literature cannot be used at all, but that one should be wary in using it.

Justified means that one justifies the proposed solution vis-à-vis the client organization. This is done firstly by describing the process through which the solution has been designed (like in every scholarly publication results are justified on the basis of a description of the research process that produced these results). But the cornerstone of the justification is an explanation of why the student thinks the designed solution will solve the problem. Furthermore, the student has to prepare a cost-benefit analysis, as the solution may solve the problem but may also be too expensive to implement. See Chapter 7.5 on justification.

Client-centred, finally, means that one deals respectfully with the client system as a whole. The client system consists of the principal, the problem owner, users of the proposed system (or people working in the redesigned business system) and other stakeholders. Of course, the principal of the project is a very important person, but both for technical and ethical reasons one should also take into account the views and interests of other stakeholders in the project.

3 Design-focused business problem-solving

3.1 Introduction

Design-focused business problem-solving (BPS) deals with improvement problems, not with pure knowledge problems. The methodology presented in this handbook aims at the design of specific solutions for specific business problems, the design of the change processes needed to realize the solutions, and the development of support within the client organizations for these designs. There are, of course, other BPS strategies and our methodology is not necessarily the best one for each and every business problem: it has a certain application domain. In this chapter we give further characterization of the design-focused, problem-solving strategy, followed by a comparison with other BPS strategies and suggestions as to when to choose which one.

Design in general, and social system design in particular, is a key ingredient of our methodology. Therefore we give some background theory on design and designing, followed by a discussion of specific issues in social system design. Ideas on social system design are strongly influenced by world views. We conclude this chapter with a brief discussion on the paradigmatic starting points of our methodology.

3.2 Characteristics of design-focused business problem-solving

The design-focused methodology for business problem-solving builds on the traditions of rational problem-solving. Systematic inquiry into problem-solving, aimed at uncovering general principles, started with the work of Herbert Simon, Alan Newell and colleagues in the 1950s (see for example Newell and Simon 1972). Their work strongly influenced cognitive science, artificial intelligence, management science and economics. A related stream of research is on organizational decision-making which was, in its formative years of the 1960s and 1970s, predominantly rational, see for example Simon (1960). An especially representative example of this approach is Kepner and Tregoe (1981). However, our design-focused methodology differs from this rational problem-solving or decision-making approach in two significant aspects.

Firstly, we see business problem-solving not as a purely technical-economic activity. The issue is not to design a smart solution, but to realize performance improvement for a certain business system. That always involves organization change, a change in organizational roles and routines, often with accompanying changes in perceptions and attitudes. With respect to organizational change we follow Tichy (1983), who maintains that significant (in his words 'strategic') planned organizational change has to be managed simultaneously in the technical, the political and the cultural subsystems, using respectively technical, political and cultural interventions. The rational problem-solving approach only deals with technical interventions. We recognize that political and cultural interventions are also needed (see Chapter 8.2). With respect to planned change there is, of course, a lot of useful organizational development literature (see for example Chin and Benne 1976; French and Bell 1999; and Cummings and Worley 2001, or literature from an organizational learning perspective (see for example Argyris 1993) .

Secondly, we relax the constraints of the so-called 'phase theorem' (Witte 1972). A defining characteristic of classical, rational problem-solving is a strict adherence to the various phases of the problem-solving process. The overall process is organized in phases, such as in the five-phase model of Kepner and Tregoe (1981): problem definition, problem specification, generation of possible solutions, testing solutions and verification (incidentally, implementation of the solution is not an issue for Kepner and Tregoe). The key demand in a classical prescriptive phase model, like the one of Kepner and Tregoe, is that any one phase should not be started before the previous one has been successfully completed. Disregarding this demand leads – in this view – to failure.

However, descriptive research, like Witte (1972) and Nutt (1984), has shown that real-life organizational problem-solving processes rarely follow a clear sequence of phases and that phased processes generally are no more successful than non-phased ones. We follow a different approach. The problem-solving process is not organized in a clear sequence of distinct *phases*, but in *process steps*. The various elements of the regulative cycle of Figure 2.1 are process steps, the scheduling of which are dependent on progress, resulting in *iterations* (jumping to previous steps) and *explorations* (jumping to subsequent steps).

For instance one may start with work on the problem definition, followed by a first problem analysis. Then an exploration of possible outline solutions may be done. Based on ideas on possible solutions one makes a more detailed problem analysis, before returning to solution design. It may even be useful to go back to problem definition on the basis of uncovered new problems or opportunities. So in our methodology there is no strict sequence of phases, but flexibility in scheduling work on the various process steps of the problem-solving process.

3.3 Problem-solving strategies

In spite of these two significant differences between our design-focused methodology to business problem-solving and the classical rational approach, we still regard our approach as a rational problem-solving one. Much of the management consulting literature also belongs to this family of approaches, see for example Albert (1980), Hicks (1995), Kubr (1996), Schaffer (1997) and Wickham (1999), as does the BPS literature by Kempen and Keizer (2006). In the family of rational approaches to problem-solving the focus of the change agent is primarily on content: the change agent has an expert role. The other major family of problem-solving strategies focuses more on process. In these approaches the role of the change agent is predominantly facilitating or coaching, see for example Schein (1969). The literature on organizational development is also largely concerned with process, see for example Chin and Benne (1976), French and Bell (1999), and Cummings and Worley (2001).

As well as distinguishing between a focus on content and a focus on process, we can also make a distinction between design approaches and development approaches to problem-solving. In the pure design approach the solution for the business problem – a redesign of roles and routines – is designed in one go and subsequently realized in one go. In the development approach on the other hand, the solution is designed and realized in a step-by-step learning approach, each step being designed and realized on the basis of what has been learnt in the previous one. One may have ideas on the general direction of the changes, but actual designing is step-by-step, design steps alternating with realization steps. A design-orientation relies on 'learning-before-doing', as opposed to the 'learning-by-doing' of the development approach (to use the words of Pisano 1994).

A well-known example of the development approach to problem-solving is Quinn's logical incrementalism (Quinn 1980). In this approach strategic change is realized in a protracted sequence of incremental changes. Lindblom's (1959) 'muddling through' may too be regarded as a development approach, the difference with Quinn maybe being that in this case it looks like 'development-by-accident', and in Quinn's case 'development-by-design'. Also the use of a small-scale, pilot implementation of changes, before an organization-wide one, may be regarded as the use of a development approach.

In practice one may want to use a combination of the design and the development approaches. A student BPS project may be one step in an overall incremental improvement strategy, with the next steps based on what has been learned in this BPS project. Also, within a student BPS project, one may want to use a combination by carefully designing a pilot implementation, followed by up-scaling the solution on the basis of lessons learnt.

The defining difference between the pure design approach and the pure development approach lies in the nature of the design and change processes. In the first case the designed end situation is realized in one go; in the second it is realized following a sequence of steps, the actions of each step being based on what has previously been learned. The defining difference between the content-focused and process-focused approaches lies in the role of the change agents. The 'theory-based' of our methodology implies that the role of the student resembles an expert role more than a process or facilitating role. In the process role, problem-solvers support their client organization to find the solution for a problem itself. In our methodology, the student works in dialogue with the client organization, to get information on the problem, to get feedback on proposed solutions and to develop acceptance for the eventual solution. Ultimately the student is responsible for the design of the solution and the accompanying change plan. In the process-focused approach, the change agents have a largely supporting or process role, helping the client system with organizing the analysis and design process and with the subsequent change process.

Literature on action research can also be relevant in this respect (see for example Clark 1972; Susman and Evered 1978; Argyris, Putnam and McLain Smith 1985; Eden and Huxham 1996; Reason and Bradbury 2001). The term action research covers a large variety of approaches (Eden and Huxham 1996). In as far as action research is research, it is aimed at solving knowledge problems and at developing general knowledge. That is done on the basis of one or a sequence of (large or small) problem-solving projects. These individual projects may use a design or development approach, but the role of the researcher is usually a facilitating one, again leaving content to others. The knowledge produced by action research is often on the change process itself, not on content, on object knowledge.

One may also mention here specific approaches for specific types of problem, like Checkland's soft systems methodology (Checkland and Scholes 1990), or TRIZ (the theory of inventive problem-solving, see for example Savransky 2000). There are differences as well as similarities between these and design-focused methodology. The discussion of such specific problem-solving approaches, however, falls outside the scope of this handbook.

3.4 Choosing a problem-solving strategy

Now there is the question of for what type of problems the design-focused methodology can be applied. As said, a problem can be defined as the result of a certain perception of a state of affairs in the real world with which one or more important stakeholders are dissatisfied. Business problems differ in content and context. In terms of the TPC model (Tichy 1983) they have technical-economic, political, and cultural components. Generally speaking, our design-focused methodology is best suited for business problems with a significant technical-economic component, while having limited political and cultural components. It can be used for ill-defined problems, but not too ill-defined, too 'wicked' problems. If the political or cultural components of the problem are dominant, a facilitating approach might be preferred. For instance, if the nature of the problem mess and the problem setting is too much like a 'garbage can' (Cohen, March and Olson 1972) with stakeholders going in and out of the setting, lack of consensus over goals and much ambiguity, a rational, design-oriented methodology may not be the best one. We do pay attention to the organizational political aspects of problem-solving, but if the setting is strongly political, the choice of adequate political interventions (or maybe even 'irrational' approaches, see Brunsson 1985) may be much more important than the rational design of strategy, structure and change, as used in our methodology.

If the problem has significant components in all three domains, like in strategic issues, a development approach might be preferred. Of course, in a student project the overall impact of the problem tends to be limited, as principals may prefer using senior management consultants rather than students to help them with significant problems. Of the more specific approaches mentioned above, Checkland's approach might be chosen if sense-making with respect to the present system is important (so a significant cultural component of the problem) and the TRIZ approach if the technical component is really dominant. Ambiguity and politics may limit the applicability of our methodology, but uncertainty and complexity do to a much lesser extent. There is, of course, in cases of strong uncertainty and complexity, the issue of 'bounded rationality' (March and Simon 1958), but as far as it is possible at all to deal with uncertainty and complexity, this methodology is suitable for it.

Another important dimension is the (anticipated) availability of data. Decision-making in business is always done on the basis of limited data, but for a design-focused approach one needs sufficient data to make rational decisions (or bounded rational decisions) on the solution and its realization. If it is reasonable to expect that such data cannot be made available, one might prefer a development approach. For a design approach one should be able to make a valid model of the future business system and one should be able to say something on its expected performance. If that cannot be done, one can use a development approach in which one designs the first step, which will be easier than producing the complete and final design, and then designs subsequent steps on the basis of experiences gained during the process.

3.5 Designs and designing

Designing is, of course, a key activity in design-focused problem-solving. Therefore in this section we give some general design theory (more can be found in Van Aken 2005b). The design theory given in this section is valid for material system designing. It is also to a large extent valid for social system designing, but there are significant differences. These will be discussed in the next chapter.

The first question, then, is: what is a design? A *design* can be defined as *a model of an entity to be realised, as an instruction for the next step in the creation process.* That entity can be an object or a process. The model can take various forms, like a drawing or a set of drawings, but can also have various other forms, such as a text, a flowchart, a scale model, a computer 3D-representation, and so on. A design is not an end in itself, but an input for the next step, which can consist of further detailing of the design in the immaterial domain of designing or of the actual realisation of the entity in the material domain.

A model is an abstraction of reality. Usually it is an abstraction of an already existing reality, but in case of a design it is a model of a possible future reality.

This design, the model of the entity to be realized, should satisfy the so-called *principle of minimal specification*. It should give *all* the information the makers of the entity need to realize this entity *as intended by the designer*. A design is not only necessary to realize the entity, it should also be sufficient. Applying the principle of minimal specification involves design decisions on what to incorporate in one's design and what not. For instance, the design of a car may not specify the yarn to be used to make the upholstery of the seats, but may leave the choice of yarn to the factory. Designers should not under-specify their designs; they should not give too little information. In material system designing over specification, giving more information than needed to realize the design usually does not do much harm; but, as we will see, in social system designing over-specification may well be harmful.

The object to be designed has to fulfil a certain function for the user. Designing can simply be defined as making a design, but a more specific definition is: '*designing is the process of determining the required function of an object to be designed, combined with making a model of it*'. One can also say that designing is developing a *functional specification* of the object to be designed, combined with making a *technical specification* of it; specifying the object in such a way that the makers of the object will have sufficient technical information to produce it.

The above definition is specific, among other things because the process of making the functional specification is regarded as being part of the design process and not as being input to it. The reason for this is that in general the designers have more insight in the technical aspects of designing and realising the new object than the principal for the design effort. In organising and planning the design process one should give much attention to the interactions between designers and the client system (interactions that are not only important in the first step of the design process, but throughout the whole design process).

Designing involves the making of three designs (see Figure 3.1):
– the *object design*, the model of the system or process to be realized;
– the *realization design*, a model of the material process through which the object design is to be realized (not always a big effort, as often a realization process is already available, or can be easily adapted to the needs of the newly designed entity);
– the *process design*, a design of the process of analysis and design that is to produce the object and realization design.

Actual designing starts from the functional specifications for the design. There are various categories of such specifications. These are listed below, in each

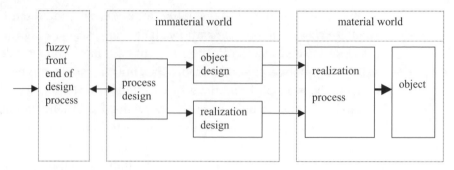

Figure 3.1   Process, object and realization design

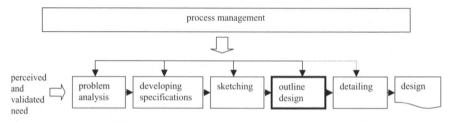

Figure 3.2   A general model for a design process

case followed by an example from the specifications for the design of a new model of freezer:

– *functional requirements*: the core of the specification in the form of performance demands on the object to be designed (freezer: temperature in the cool space can be controlled for the interval 10°C – minus 10°C);
– *user requirements*: specific requirements from the viewpoint of the user (freezer: easy to defrost);
– *boundary conditions*: to be met unconditionally (freezer: the system will use a 220 V power supply);
– *design restrictions*: preferred solution space (freezer: the new model should preferably use the same compressor as the existing one).

In Figure 3.2 a general model is given of a design process. This is but one of the many possible models of a design process (see for example Evbuonwan, Sivaloganathan and Jebb 1996, for a survey of design process models, and also Van Aken 2005b). This one is developed to show the basic steps in the design process and to show the functions of (design) process management. This general model of a design process can be regarded as a detailing of the design part of the regulative cycle, given in figure 2.1. The problem definition of figure 2.1 is an input to the design process. The process step 'analysis and diagnosis' is broken down into 'problem analysis' and 'developing specifications' and the step 'plan of action' is broken down into 'sketching', 'outline design' and 'detailing'.

The process of figure 3.2 has as its input a 'perceived and validated need' of a certain target group. It is not the need itself that is the input for the design process, but a perception of that need, which is validated by the principal and seen as sufficiently worthwhile to invest the required resources to design and realize the object in question. The term 'perceived' is also used because one may need further analysis (and discussions with the problem owner and the intended users) to gain further insight of that need.

Another input to the design process is design knowledge, which usually primarily consists of object knowledge. One has public design knowledge, acquired among other things through literature and by hiring well-trained and educated designers. One also has proprietary design knowledge, for example acquired through buying licences, collaboration with organisations having valuable design knowledge, and research and development.

In figure 3.2 the overall design process is broken down into a number of sub-processes or process steps, each of which can be further detailed. The arrows above the sub-processes refer to *iterations* and *explorations* (as already mentioned in chapter 3.2): iterations by going to a previous step, for example if more information is needed from that step; and explorations by briefly jumping to a step further on in the process to explore possible design solutions. *Process management* has the task of scheduling the work on the various process steps and the iterations and explorations. Figure 3.2 is not a *phase model*, in which the phases follow a fixed sequence, but a *process step model*: the overall process is broken down into essential process steps, while work on each of the steps is controlled by process management

A key element of the model in figure 3.2 is the *outline design* (also called the conceptual design). This outline design is not an informal sketch, but a formal design containing all the design decisions with respect to the key design dilemmas. The intention is that many iterations and explorations may take place during sketching and drawing up the outline design, but that the outline design itself should be fairly robust in order that the time- and money-consuming detailing can be done without further iterations. Therefore, the iteration-exploration line between 'outline design' and 'detailing' design is dotted.

The basic iterations in the actual design process are *synthesis-evaluation iterations* (see Figure 3.3). In fact, the essence of all designing consists of two steps:

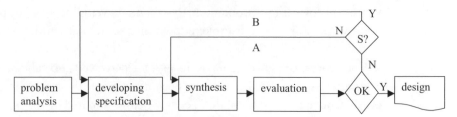

Figure 3.3   Synthesis-evaluation iterations (loop A) and specification-design iterations (loop B) are started if the answer to question S ('change specifications?') is 'yes'

1. one *synthesises* in the immaterial world of communication, with drawings and texts of the entity to be realized; followed by
2. an *evaluation* of the expected performance of that entity against specifications 'on paper', that is in this same immaterial world.

If the evaluation does not produce a satisfactory result, a new or adapted synthesis is made and re-evaluated. If this iteration process eventually fails to produce a satisfactory solution, a second type of iteration is started: *specification-design iterations* (loop B in figure 3.3). In consultation with the principal (and possibly other members of the client system) the functional specifications are adapted and a design process (synthesis-evaluation iterations) is started to see whether it is possible to meet the new specifications. If not, the specifications are again re-adapted.

In line with these two basis steps, key design knowledge consists firstly of alternative tested *general solution concepts* (see chapter 4.2), which designers can use as 'design models' for making specific variants for their specific design problems, and secondly of *methods to evaluate alternative designs 'on paper'*. For instance, engineers have to master a lot of mathematics because they so often use mathematical methods to evaluate the performance of their designs 'on paper', in the immaterial world of designing. The fundamental difference between the design approach and the development approach, discussed in Chapter 3.3, is that in the first case the evaluation of designs is done in the immaterial world of designing, and in the second case in the material world of action.

Sometimes one does not have sufficient object knowledge to be able to evaluate a design in the immaterial world of drawings and texts (which may be the case in radical design). In that case one may want to make a material prototype of the design and to evaluate the performance of that realized design against specifications in the material world. This may also involve an iterative procedure. The use of material prototypes to evaluate designs can be seen as a development approach to designing, like the development approach to problem-solving discussed in Chapter 3.3.

A design process should produce an object design and, if needed, a realization design. A professional design process itself should be executed on the basis of an explicit process design. That process design specifies in principle the *undisturbed process*. It is a model of what will happen if all goes according to plan. Of course, in actual realization of the process design there will be various disturbances, like delays in finding solutions to certain design problems, changes in the functional specification because the external world and its competitive conditions will not stand still during the design process, or increasing insight in the validated need or in the potential of technology which triggers changes in specifications or plans. On the one hand it is the task of process management to deal with such disturbances in a kind of management-by-exception, and on the other hand a process design should have some in-built flexibility (with for example buffers in time) to deal with disturbances.

3.6 Designing social systems

Business problem-solving involves social system designing: a business system having performance problems is redesigned and the redesigned system is introduced in order to improve its performance.

Some hold that social system design, or social engineering, is impossible. One cannot create social systems with essentially immaterial properties on the basis of design, as one can create material systems like buildings or machines on the basis of design. However, business practice shows that social system design *is* possible: in business it is common practice to redesign departmental structures, individual positions or work procedures and to introduce these redesigns successfully in the organization. Planned change is feasible. Still, it is true that one cannot create social systems on the basis of design in the same way that one can create material ones. So, in the context of sound BPS it is worthwhile to have a close look at social system design, to see what exactly is designed and realized, and to what extent social system design differs from the design of buildings or machines.

In the first place social system design only has real meaning if it is *realizable*. Anybody can produce a design, in other words make a model or a drawing of something; a child can design a flying skyscraper by drawing wings onto a tall building, and Jules Verne has designed a submarine and a rocket to the moon. Realizable design, on the other hand, is making a model of an entity that *technically can be realized on the basis of that model.* Social system design has only real meaning if it is possible to create a social system *on the basis of that design.* That is exactly the purpose of the redesign of a business system in the course of a BPS project.

In the previous chapter we discussed design theory for material system designing. As said, this theory is also largely valid for social system design, but there are significant differences. There is an important technical difference in the design process itself and a more fundamental difference in the realization process.

With respect to the design process itself, the synthesis step in social system design, that is making a model of a business system to be realized in the form of charts, flow diagrams and texts, can be quite similar to the synthesis step in material system design. For instance, the design of a fully automated manufacturing system in the form of a flow chart can be quite similar, even to the extent of using similar symbols, to a flow chart designed for a manual procedure to settle insurance claims. There are more problems in the evaluation step, however. Because the behaviour of social systems is not governed by law like causal relations as is typically the case in material systems (see for example Numagami 1998), the performance of designed social systems is much more difficult to predict on paper than normally is the case in material system design. (See Chapter 7.3 on evaluation in business system design.)

A more fundamental difference in design and realization between material and social systems is not in the design process itself but in the realization of the system. The material system is realized by makers such as building contractors or workshops, through material processes using raw materials and components. They usually get only very limited 'realization freedom'; the material system is largely realized as designed, the realizers having in principle only realization freedom outside the scope of the specifications in the design (the principle of minimal specification).

In contrast, a social system has essentially immaterial aspects and components. It is made and driven by the thoughts and feelings of the human actors in the system. A redesigned social system is realized by these actors by changing their ideas on their social systems. These ideas can very well and to a large extent be influenced by that redesign, but they are not determined by it: the 'makers' of the social system typically have quite a lot of realization freedom.

In social system design the social system is realized on the basis of a design made by people in a change agent role, such as management, specialized staff, management consultants, or students doing a BPS project. We will call this design the *first redesign*. We call it a redesign because it usually is a redesign of an existing business system, and because typically it is a contextualized, redesigned version of one or more general solution concepts from the literature. This first redesign gives a representation of the new formal system.

We call the design made by change agents the *first redesign* because it is always followed by a *second redesign*. This second redesign is an *appropriation* of the new formal system by the organizational actors concerned (see DeSanctis and Poole (1994) on the concept of appropriation). We call it a redesign because it is a redesign by the actors themselves of their existing roles and routines, which always involves much more detail than the formal system gives. It is also a redesign because not only does it involve a further detailing of the formal system, but typically also an adaptation to individual circumstances, personal ideas, and preferences (to the extent that the situation and the monitoring by the change agents permit this realization freedom).

As discussed in Chapter 2.1, planned organizational change involves a change phase in which the formal organization is changed, followed by a learning phase in which the organizational actors learn to operate in the new system and produce as far as possible the intended performance. It is especially in this learning phase that the second redesign operates: the actors learn their new roles and routines and adapt during this process – unconsciously or consciously – the formal roles and routines. In this phase the necessary new informal organization emerges.

Social systems are not designed for and realized by machines or robots, but for human actors – individuals and groups – with self-organizing and self-control faculties. Typically these actors experience much freedom in the realization of their new social system. For the change agents this has advantages as well as disadvantages. The advantages include the fact that not each and every detail of the new business system has to be designed by the designers, as is the case for a system designed for robots. Much of the detailing can be left to self-organization and self-control. The disadvantages include that the designers have much less control over the realization of their system than do the designers of material systems.

Because of this second redesign designers of social systems have to make conscious use of the principle of minimal specification. They should only specify what the actors in the system really need to know to create an effective and efficient business system. In practice designers tend to over-specify their designs, which may lead to an induced low willingness to change (see Chapter 8.2), or to a rejection by the actors in the system of those elements they regard as over-specified.

Less control over the realization of a social system redesign may be counter-acted by monitoring the development of the new system and by taking action on dysfunctional differences between the unfolding reality and the redesign. Even so, control over the new business system is limited. A social system is at the same time an *artefact*, created through the interventions and designs by owners, managers, designers and other influential stakeholders, and a *natural system*, developing gradually over time through the interactions among its members and through their constant experimentation and learning. A formal redesign of a social system is not only a starting point for its subsequent realization but also for further development after the initial realization. So, next to the 'technical' difference in the design process, the fundamental difference between material system design and realization on the one hand, and social system design and realization on the other, includes both the vagaries of the second redesign by the human actors in the system *and* the subsequent further development of it.

Business systems are seldom pure social systems, but usually hybrid ones for example socio-technical systems: if the social component is limited, such as in a strongly formalized scheduling system for the shop floor of a factory, business system design may be quite similar to the design of material systems. In terms of the above given discussion, one can say that the second redesign has only limited impact on the realization of the system. If, however, the social component is stronger, the designers have to put more effort in managing that second redesign by intense communication on the content of the first redesign and by motivating the actors in the system to make their second redesign in accordance with this first redesign. If, for instance using the example of the scheduling system, the operators have quite some freedom to change the schedules presented to them through the system, the change agents have much work to do to realize that those changes are still in accordance with the principles of the system.

3.7 Paradigmatic starting points

Design is based on *knowledge* of a certain segment of the existing *reality*, and generates knowledge to create a new segment of reality. Therefore it entails *epistemological* issues, concerning ideas on the nature of knowledge, and *onto-logical* issues, concerning the nature of reality.

Epistemology defines the criteria by which warranted knowledge is possible: what are the origins, nature and limits of scientific knowledge (Johnson and Durberly 2000). So epistemology can be regarded as the 'Science of science'.

But this generates a problem of circularity (Johnson and Durberly 2000): if this Science (with an upper case S) is to set criteria for judging science (with a lower case s), what science is there to set the criteria for Science? **Science** with a bold upper case **S**? Clearly one cannot escape from this circularity. This means that epistemological – and because of this also ontological – positions ultimately rest on a world view, set of paradigmatic starting points, and a kind of philosophical axiom, which are hard to debate due to a lack of common ground. This section will give a brief exposé of the paradigmatic starting points for writing this handbook.

In material system design, like in the natural sciences, differences in paradigmatic starting points do not play a significant role and, therefore, typically remain tacit. Most engineers and natural scientists hold world views that resemble some variants of realism. These claim that there exists a material reality, independent from observers (an ontological position), and that it is possible to develop objective knowledge on this reality by observation and reasoning (an epistemological position).

However, in social system design paradigmatic differences do matter. People in business systems – in managerial, operational and even professional roles – tend to hold similar views with respect to social and material systems. In that case the organization, the department, and the position of the boss, is of a similar objective reality as the factory building or a box of rivets. In this way they *reify* their organization, make it a material thing (Silverman 1970). They, especially the managers among them, tend to combine this world view with the ideals of the Enlightenment: one can not only obtain objective knowledge on reality, but one can also use this knowledge to change reality for the better, to 'make' reality, not only with respect to material reality, but also with respect to social reality, like the reality of an organization. This view often is characterized as being *modernistic* (see for example Hatch 1997).

Our world view is different. Following Searle (1995) we hold different assumptions for material reality and social reality. With respect to the material world, our discussion on problem-solving, social system design and organizational change is based on the views of *critical realism* (Bhaskar 1986), and with respect to the social world, on the views of *social constructivism* (Berger and Luckman 1967; Searle 1995). With respect to the material world, realism holds that there is a material reality, independent from the observer, on which one can obtain knowledge through observation and reasoning. But critical realism asserts that this knowledge cannot be objective, because all observations are concept-laden and fallible and inductive reasoning from observations is inconclusive. Nevertheless, 'critical' also means that one can make critical judgements on the validity of knowledge claims on the basis of 'transactions', or interactions with reality. ('Critical' further means being critical with respect to power issues in discussing the social world. Although certainly not unimportant for organizations, the discussion of such issues falls outside the scope of this handbook).

With respect to the social world, our ontological position follows *social constructivism*. One can also say that with respect to social reality we hold an *interpretative or symbolic* world view (Hatch 1997). Social institutions such as marriage, contracts, money, the fatherland and also the organization are *not* realities independent from the observer but exist because, and only because, people (collectively) *think* that they exist. Such realities are socially constructed through intense and prolonged communication on the institution in question. The discussion on the second redesign in the previous section is in fact a discussion producing the social construction of the new organization.

One can obtain knowledge on this social world through the interpretation of the communications and actions of its members. Also, this knowledge cannot be objective, and with respect to this knowledge one can make critical judgements on its validity.

The material and social worlds coexist. Artefacts, such as goods produced by a company, have a dual nature as they are part of both the material and the social world. On the one hand they are part of the material world, subjected to natural laws. On the other hand they are part of the social world, as they depend upon our beliefs for being an artefact of a particular kind and purpose.

In social system design paradigmatic starting points do matter. Ignoring the socially constructed nature of the organization decreases the insight in both the possibilities *and* impossibilities for changing organizational realities. On the one hand the reification of the organization can induce one to constrain ones actions by organizational relations and boundaries in the same absolute way as material walls and staircases constrain physical movements, thus underestimating the potential to change organizational realities through communication. On the other hand one may not see the 'unbearable lightness' of the *collective* construction of social reality by overestimating the possibilities of change. One may think that presenting a new organization chart will produce that new organization, as easily as presenting a drawing of a new layout of an office floor to a building contractor will produce the shifting of some walls. Awareness of different world views on organizations really *is* important for organization design, and thus for business problem-solving.

4   Theory-based business problem-solving

4.1   Theory-based problem analysis and solution design

The business problem-solving (BPS) methodology presented in this handbook is theory-based. As said in Chapter 1, problem analysis and solution design should be based on comprehensive, critical and creative use of the literature. Business problem-solving can be informed by many sources of knowledge and inspiration, but an important one is the scholarly literature on organization and management and on the various business functions like marketing, operations, product development and management accounting. We will see in Chapter 5 that an important – and often quite difficult – aspect of problem definition in BPS is to define it as a special type of problem within a business system. Students have to do this in order to be able to focus their literature search on the right type of problem and business system (as there is, of course, no literature on their specific problem).

Next to the scholarly literature, there is also management literature, written by practitioners for practitioners (see Chapter 11.2). This literature can be an important source of inspiration for solution design. However, often its major weakness is the limited evidence given. That makes it difficult for students to make evaluations of designs based on this type of literature on paper. Or, in other words, it is difficult to judge how the proposed business solution will work in their specific setting.

The scholarly literature also has its limitations. A large segment of it has a quantitative nature and is, therefore, strongly reductionistic. This type of literature can be quite useful to get a rough idea of the performance of certain general business solutions. However it gives only very limited guidance for actual solution design.

Most scholarly literature, quantitative and qualitative alike, is descriptive rather than prescriptive. Descriptive literature focuses on *that what is*, rather than on *that what can be* to improve performance. It tends to focus on analysis, the causes of phenomena, the causes of possible malfunctions or of less than satisfactory performance, but not on possible solutions. Still, scholarly literature on management can be a rich source of knowledge for BPS, see Chapter 6.3. However, because of its largely descriptive nature, business designers often have to use the above-mentioned management literature as well. Even if such literature provides limited evidence, its solution orientation can provide valuable inspiration for solution design.

Descriptive knowledge can be used in a conceptual way, to give general enlightenment on the issues in question. For solution design one would also like to have prescriptive knowledge in order to use such knowledge in a more direct, instrumental way (see Pelz 1978, on the distinction between conceptual and instrumental use of knowledge). Prescriptive knowledge tends to be mistrusted by academics, either because of the limited evidence given with the prescriptions or because the development of prescriptive knowledge is seen as rather un-academic, better left to practitioners. However, in our view, the development of valid prescriptive knowledge, or design knowledge, by scholarly research can strongly contribute to effective business problem-solving (Van Aken 2004; 2005a). Such research, which may be called design science research, is the subject of this chapter. The conceptual use of present day scholarly literature is important for BPS, but design science research in our field can strongly enhance the usefulness of scholarly literature for BPS.

4.2 Solution concepts for business problem-solving

Following Van Aken (2004) one can make a distinction between *explanatory sciences*, like the natural sciences and most social sciences, and *design sciences*, like medicine and engineering. The core mission of an explanatory science is to develop valid knowledge to describe, explain and predict empirical phenomena within the scope of the science in question. Students of an explanatory science are trained to become *researchers* in order to be able to add to the knowledge base of their discipline. Research in an explanatory science may be regarded as a quest for understanding, a quest for truth. It focuses on the immaterial world of knowledge.

On the other hand, the core mission of a design science is the development of valid knowledge, which can be used by professionals in the field in question to *design* solutions to their field problems (hence the term 'design science').

Students of a design science are trained to become *professionals*, able to solve field problems. Research in a design science can be seen as a quest for improving the human condition. It focuses on the material world of action and material results.

One of the typical research products of an explanatory science is the causal model, explaining – preferably in quantitative terms – a phenomenon of interest in terms of some independent variables. Such models and other descriptive knowledge can be used to understand the nature and causes of problems, which can be a great help in solving them. However, under-standing – the result of *analysis* – only goes halfway towards solving the prob-lem. The other half consists of designing alternative solutions, and choosing and implementing one. The typical research product of a design science, sup-porting that solution and implementation design, is the *technological rule*, respectively the *solution concept* (see Van Aken 2004; 2005a).

A technological rule is a chunk of knowledge, connecting a certain interven-tion or system in a certain context with a certain outcome. More specifically, the *logic* of the technological rule is: if you want to achieve Y in setting Z, than do X (or something like X). This logic is concise, but the actual full description of a technological rule may take a full report or article or even a book.

The core of the technological rule is the X, the actual intervention or sys-tem to be implemented. That X is a general *solution concept*, a type of solution to a type of problem. In designing solutions to field problems, professionals may choose one solution concept out of several and then design a specific variant of that general solution concept, adapted to the specific requirements of their specific field problem (like a civil engineer chooses a *type* of bridge before designing a specific one). Examples of solution concepts in organiza-tion design are the functional structure, the product-oriented structure and the matrix structure. In inventory control one has various inventory control systems from which to choose, and in competitive strategy various ways to follow a differentiation strategy. These solution concepts can be turned into technological rules on the basis of their advantages and disadvantages in vari-ous settings. A full formulation of such a technological rule gives for a solution concept X the objectives the application of the solution concept would serve (the Y), and for which situations (the Z) the rule would be valid.

The most powerful technological rule or solution concept is the field-tested and grounded one. 'Field tested' means that the solution concept is sufficiently tested in its intended field of application, and 'grounded' means that it is known why the use of the solution concept produces its intended outcome.

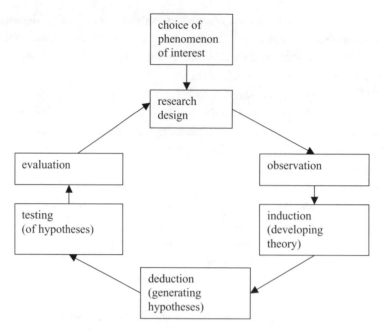

Figure 4.1   The empirical cycle (after De Groot 1969)

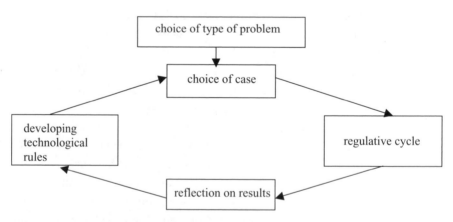

Figure 4.2   The learning or reflective cycle (after Van Aken 2004)

4.3 Developing knowledge for business problem-solving

Sound BPS uses the results from descriptive research, research based on the paradigm of the explanatory sciences and from prescriptive or design-orientated research, and research based on the paradigm of the design sciences.

Research based on the paradigm of the explanatory sciences usually follows the so-called *empirical cycle* (see figure 4.1). One chooses a phenomenon of interest, makes a research design, makes empirical observations on the basis of that research design, develops via induction a theory, deduces from that theory empirically verifiable observations (testable hypotheses), and then tests these hypotheses. Testing can either confirm the theory or lead to a rejection or adaptation of the theory. If not fully confirmed, a new cycle can be started to further develop the theory. Almost all literature on methodology in the social sciences is concerned with this empirical cycle.

Research based on the paradigm of the design sciences, aimed at developing prescriptive knowledge in the form of (field-tested and grounded) technological rules or solution concepts, does not usually follow the empirical cycle, but instead the learning or *reflective cycle*, see figure 4.2 (Van Aken 2004).

The basis of the reflective cycle is a business problem-solving activity, following the regulative cycle discussed in Chapter 2.2. The reflective cycle consists of choosing a type of business problem, solving that problem through the regulating cycle, reflecting on the results with the aim of learning from this project for similar projects, establishing preliminary technological rules, and then starting a new project dealing with the same type of problem. The core of the reflective cycle is the reflection step. In this step cross-case analyzes are used to generate general knowledge by removing the case-specific elements from the results of the cases.

Of course, not only academics can produce valid technological rules and solution concepts. Like in engineering and medicine, professionals can also reflect on their cases, do cross-case analyses (using their own cases and cases from the literature) and can in this way generate valid design knowledge.

Part II

The problem-solving project

In this part we discuss the various aspects of the business problem-solving project, following the steps of the regulative cycle: problem definition, analysis and diagnosis, plan of action, intervention and evaluation.

5 Intake and orientation

5.1 General setup

The business problem-solving (BPS) project starts with an *intake process* and an *orientation process*. In terms of the regulative cycle, intake and orientation should together be regarded as the 'problem definition' step. In terms of a consulting project, intake should be regarded as the contracting phase. A successful intake process results in a written initial assignment. Based upon that initial assignment, work within a company begins with a relatively brief orientation phase. For a nine-month BPS project, the orientation phase should take no more than four weeks. Orientation will result in a further detailing of the technical content of the assignment, but typically not of its contractual conditions. Orientation results in a definitive project proposal, including the definitive assignment.

A typical project proposal discusses six issues:

1. *The problem context*: a brief description of the company in question and the background of the project (see section 5.4).
2. *The problem statement*: the problem statement is a crucial part of the project proposal. The problem statement is preferably accompanied by a preliminary analysis of causes and effects, as that may support the 'naming and framing' of the problem and the design of the project approach (see section 5.5).
3. *The assignment*: this section of the project proposal contains the deliverables that will be generated by the project (see section 5.6).
4. *The project approach*: the student should design both a conceptual and a technical approach to solve the problem (see section 5.7).
5. *The costs of the project*: the expected costs of the project should be specified as much as possible (see section 5.8)

6. *The organization of the project*: the proposal should make clear who is the
   principal of the project and who else will be involved and how (see section
   5.8)

The definitive assignment, which is drawn up at the end of the orientation
phase, is usually definitive indeed. However, the subsequent diagnosis and
redesign may uncover unforeseen difficulties or opportunities, making it useful
or even necessary to renegotiate the assignment with the principal(s).

This chapter proceeds with a discussion of the externally executed intake
and internally executed orientation. Whereas the intake yields an initial assignment, the orientation phase results in a definitive assignment, encapsulated
in a project proposal. Sections 5.4 to 5.8 discuss each of the components of
a typical project proposal, as listed above. In this chapter we usually assume
an individual project of about six to eight months. Section 5.9 addresses BPS
projects in different formats. The final section of this chapter contains an
example of a project proposal.

5.2 The intake process

The intake process starts with an initial contact with a company representative,
exploring the possibilities of a BPS project. The choice for a company to be
approached can be based on a variety of reasons. Students or their supervisors
may have had prior contact with the company. Interest in the company may
also be based upon an external exploration. In either case, the prospects of
interesting a company are higher if one proposes a specific – but not too
narrowly defined – topic for a potential project. If the contact is successful, an
appointment for a first meeting is made.

The intake meeting is prepared by a fairly comprehensive *external exploration* in order to become a knowledgeable discussion partner. The external
exploration consists of a preliminary investigation of the organization and its
industry, based upon external sources. In our experience, a relationship can
often be found between developments and problems in the industry and internal business problems. Therefore the external exploration should determine
relationships between current developments in the industry and the wider
organization, and the topic that one intends to focus upon.

Roughly speaking, current developments in the industry have to be listed,
as well as the competitive position of the company within the industry, current
developments within the organization, and possible relationships between
the issues found and the topic of study. Sources to obtain the aforementioned

---

Box 5.1   Example of the use of an external exploration

A research and development (R&D) department of a company producing domestic appliances had problems with the return on innovation. The department had to transfer innovations to regional divisions that had to produce and sell them. The regional divisions generally accepted only minor improvements of the existing products, so the return on innovation was mostly determined by the minor improvements. A student was asked to come up with proposals to increase the return on innovation. In his external exploration the student found that the board was planning to change the organization in such a way that the R&D department would only be responsible for major innovations, while the regional divisions became responsible for the minor improvements. Given the find that the regional divisions tended to reject major innovations, the future of the R&D department was in danger. It made the initial request to the student a strategically very important issue. Maybe too important to leave it to a student.

---

information include: industry associations, journals, libraries, handbooks, the Chamber of Commerce, government offices, and the Internet. Information from all these sources generally has to be analyzed and structured to be useful for the external exploration.

The external exploration may extend into the orientation phase. In that case, the external exploration is not confined to the environment of the corporate organization, but may include the internal environment of a department. An in-depth study of the department itself is never part of the external exploration. Box 5.1 presents an example of such an external exploration.

The first *intake meeting* serves a variety of purposes. One of the goals is to get acquainted with each other. Moreover, global information about the company (such as organization charts, annual reports) and the academic education of the student may be shared. Also a suitable supervisor from the company for the project must be appointed. This is not necessarily the principal, but these roles may be overlapping. Yet the most important purpose of the first intake meeting is that it should provide sufficient material for an initial assignment and initial project proposal.

During the intake meeting the principal may explain the problem mess that the company faces. On the basis of this first introduction to the problem mess, a preliminary agreement is made to make this business problem the focus of the further internal exploration. This is the first and best moment for the student to be critical on the business problem and the assignment to analyse and solve it. The business problem(s) should match the interests of the student. Furthermore, in order to engage in a BPS project instead of a research project, the problem should be performance-related (see chapter 2.1). Finally, the potential assignment should be feasible. In the examples, given in box 5.2,

Box 5.2　Examples of business problems and corresponding assignments

Example 1: A building company in the south-east of the Netherlands wants to obtain the ISO 9001 quality certificate. This certificate is a kind of charter that business processes are controlled by to ensure their quality is at a satisfactory level. For the building company it would be a good advertising instrument too. The company proposed the following assignment for the student: make sure that we obtain the ISO 9001 certificate.

Example 2: A small company in the Netherlands of about 80 employees develops and produces moulds and synthetic products based on these moulds. There are three main departments involved in the problem: innovation, manufacturing, and quality control. The quality manager wants the student to make another prioritization of business objectives. In the current trade-off, logistic objectives have a higher priority than quality objectives. That should be changed.

Example 3: A motor vehicle company wants to conduct an exploratory study on the future activities and organization of the quality control department. Due to environmental demands like high flexibility, high quality, low prices from the side of the customer, and a changing labour market such as more staff on an academic level, this exploratory study was necessary. A student was asked to execute the exploratory study.

Example 4: ABC Research, having around 300 employees, is conducting macroeconomic and econometric research for governmental agencies. Typical projects are evaluations of governmental policies. Because many researchers leave the organization, there is a problem of maintaining knowledge on required levels in the organization. Moreover, research meetings to share knowledge have been cancelled because of a lack of interest. The student was asked to develop a knowledge-sharing infrastructure.

we will address some feasibility problems. These problems should be discussed with the principal; often they can be solved. If not, the student can better refuse the proposed assignment.

From the first example, we can learn that assignments must be organizationally feasible. For example, students cannot be responsible for obtaining an ISO 9001 certificate, since they cannot commit the necessary organizational resources to do the work and they cannot do it alone. At best, a student can facilitate the course of action required to obtain the certificate. Moreover, in the first example the assignment focuses on a solution right away. In sound BPS work one should first look at the underlying performance-related problem first, as this prevents producing a solution that is developed for something that is not really a problem, or that alternative solutions are overlooked (see also chapter 8.5).

In the second example there is also a responsibility problem. Clearly, this problem falls outside the responsibility of the quality manager. The project should be formulated on a higher organizational level, where the different organization goals come together and a trade-off can be made. In the third example, there may be a 'technical' feasibility problem. It is questionable whether the necessary information can be obtained. If this information is not available in the organization itself or within the industry, it is impossible to conduct the study, since literature will not provide insights for such a specific situation. Actually, in our view, only the problem in the fourth example is suitable for a student to explore. Yet even in that case the student has to avoid the trap of jumping to a solution.

To summarize, there are a lot of requirements for a suitable business problem. It is important:
– to start with a business problem instead of an assignment to develop a given solution;
– to have a principal with full responsibility for the problem;
– that it is feasible to collect the necessary data;
– that the project is feasible within the given amount of time;
– that the project is relevant for the company;
– that the supervisors have suitable knowledge and skills.

Decision-making on problem statement and assignment are crucial for eventual project success. Therefore it is important that the above given requirements are met.

5.3 The orientation process

When the company and the student with his or her supervisors agree upon the initial problem statement and assignment, the student can start with the *internal orientation* process. During the internal orientation the business problem is discussed with important stakeholders in the problem. Typically, five to ten interviews are conducted with people who are responsible for the (solution of the) problem and people who are confronted with the problem. The primary purpose of these interviews is to add other perspectives to the preliminary formulated problem, to be able to assess its scope and depth. However, more descriptive information can also be gained, for example regarding the primary business processes in the organization, and it can be examined whether required information is available in the organization. Furthermore, the organizational support for investigating the problem and finding a solution can be assessed and increased.

During the first step of the regulative cycle the student must actively listen to the organization members, who tell their stories related to the topic of the study. The style of questions is still very exploratory at this stage of the study.

The preliminary problem, discussed in the intake meeting, will be a starting point for the interviews. It may be discussed whether there really is a problem, and if so, why it exists and has not already been solved within the organization. Further, one may ask what are thought to be the root causes of the problem, what types of solutions would be possible, what solutions have been tried, and why these were not successful. The effort that has already been put into solving a problem can be an indication of the difficulty of the problem.

The data and opinions that are gathered in the interviews held during the orientation process are the basis for the definitive project proposal. Based upon the project proposal, a meeting should be organized to take 'final' decisions on the project. The principal, the company supervisor, the university supervisor(s), the student, and possibly other important stakeholders should join this meeting. At the meeting it should be decided to continue the project in line with the proposal or to adapt the proposal.

5.4 Describing the problem context

In the introduction to this chapter we stated that a project proposal usually contains six elements: (1) a description of the problem context; (2) the problem definition; (3) the assignment; (4) the project approach; (5) the costs of the project; and (6) the organization of the project. This section and the next sections will subsequently discuss each of these elements of a project proposal. Section 5.9 presents an example of a project proposal containing these elements.

The first element of a project proposal is a brief description of the company in question, including its mission in terms of products and services, customer groups and main competitors, its size, internal structure and geographical distribution, and its history. Furthermore, the more immediate context of the problem is discussed. This part of the proposal does not give much new information to the principal(s) of the project, but it forces students to get some idea of the problem context and shows that they have understood that context.

5.5 Problem definition

The problem definition is a crucial part of the project proposal. If a BPS project runs into trouble, it is often traceable to shortcomings of the *problem statement.* Therefore, the problem statement should be developed carefully. A problem definition is not a given, but a choice made by the student together with the principal and other stakeholders. This is not always straightforward. In practice a student will be faced with a problem mess on a particular topic.

In general, a problem can be defined as a state of affairs in the real world with which important stakeholders are dissatisfied, while they believe that things can be improved. Dissatisfaction is a necessary, but not sufficient condition for a problem. There are many unsatisfactory situations in the world that are not defined as problems, because people feel that they cannot be solved. In order to count as a problem, stakeholders should believe that the unsatisfactory situation can be solved within a reasonable amount of time, spending a reasonable amount of resources.

This handbook is predominantly concerned with *performance-related business problems.* In business problem-solving the 'unsatisfactory state of affairs' is usually an unsatisfactory performance. The performance indicator in question can be financial, like too high costs of purchasing or the unsatisfactory profitability of a certain product line. But it can also be an operational performance that does not meet an aspiration level, like the throughput time of production in a given department, or a high level of obsolete stock, or an unsatisfactory brand recognition in some markets. The problem may have direct consequences for the quality, flexibility, availability, or costs of the output of the organization on an operational level; or on a more strategic level for the market share, net profit, return on investment, or the percentage of sales coming from new products/services, number of patents.

In this handbook we restrict the use of the term 'problem' to refer to an unsatisfactory performance, or a state-of-affairs that is directly related to an unsatisfactory performance. The problem statement should, therefore, refer to either business performance that is unsatisfactory, or a state-of-affairs that is undesirable because it leads to lower performance. In both cases the problem statement should address the strategic relevance of the problem, that is, the relevance of the problem from the perspective of the business objectives. A problem statement may also contain a reference to potential causes of the problem, as long as it is made clear what is the problem and what is a potential cause. Finally, we want to stress that in a BPS project, the problem is not a question, nor can it be formulated as a question, because a BPS project is not oriented at knowledge problems.

The setting of the problem definition typically is a *problem mess* (Ackoff 1981a), a combination of perceptions of reality, of value judgements on the basis of those perceptions and of powerful or less powerful people making those judgements. A problem for a BPS project is a choice out of such a problem mess, a selection of one or more issues to work on. Notice that by selecting a business problem and formulating an assignment related to this business problem an important demarcation is made: only symptoms, causes and solutions with respect to the business problem will be taken into account.

In order to make a selection, the problem mess needs to be *represented*. Therefore, the information gained during the intake and orientation has to be structured and conveniently presented. The format we propose is a *cause and effect diagram*, in which the more symptomatic phenomena are posited on the right side of the diagram and the causes on the left side. An 'informal' cause and effect tree provides more freedom to relate causes and effects and is better able to display the chronology of causes and effects than a more formal format like Ishikawa diagrams (Ishikawa 1990). Figure 5.1 presents an example of such a diagram based upon the orientation within a retailer of second-hand office equipment. A cause and effect diagram generally shows a mess of symptoms that is created by a mess of causes. Of course, the cause and effect tree that is constructed during the orientation phase is preliminary in nature and rather unreliable. Its main function is to help select a problem from the problem mess that will be considered as a business problem in the following phases of the regulative cycle. Similar criteria as mentioned in the intake session can be used to make such a choice.

Selecting a business problem at the very right side of the cause and effect diagram normally increases the relevance of the study, but decreases the feasibility. In the example presented in figure 5.1 the performance that was ultimately at stake was the profit margin of the products that were sold. However, if that is chosen as the problem, a very broad scope of causes has to be considered, relating to marketing, quality, stock levels, purchasing, and information systems. Furthermore, the actual diagnosis will probably uncover many causes which are not yet represented in the diagram. In general, the availability of information on such a large scale may pose a serious problem and such a broad scope of knowledge and skills of the supervisors cannot always be expected. Moreover, the problem may not be completely within the span of control of the principal, and the probability of political issues regarding the problem increases.

Instead of focusing on the profit margins, one may also choose one of the intermediate issues as the business problem. In discussion with the principal either the costs or the price level may be chosen as the problem, or, if these problems are still considered too broad, one may propose to focus on one of the underlying causes: the costs of stocks, the costs of the replacement of

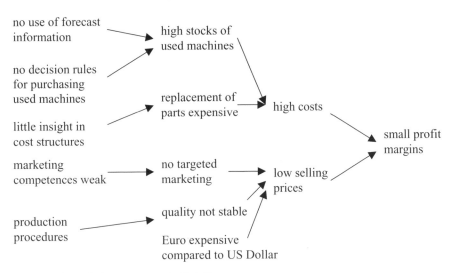

Figure 5.1   Example of a preliminary cause-and-effect diagram

parts, the quality problem or the marketing problem. Further analysis will probably show that each of those problems is caused by a network of more detailed causes. Scoping the BPS project by choosing one of those issues as the central business problem (and leaving aside the other parts of the cause and effect diagram) makes the problem more feasible, but still relevant from the perspective of business performance.

Selecting the problem at the very left side of the diagram increases the feasibility of the research, but may decrease the relevance for the company. The impact of the left-hand-side factors on business performance may be limited. Other important factors may be overlooked when the problem is selected on the very left side. The problem that is chosen should be relevant in the light of the mission and the strategy of the company. At least, the value of solving the problem should exceed the value of the resources that have to be spent on the project.

A student may also be confronted with a predefined problem: the principal has already decided what the problem to be solved should be. Although this is a really important input for the problem definition, students should not unquestionably execute what has been presented to them. They should analyze whether this is a good problem definition, given the interests and the priorities of the principal and of the organization as a whole.

Selecting a business problem – aided by a preliminary cause and effect diagram or not – entails a process of *naming and framing* (Schön 1983). By using existing concepts for naming the problem and its causes, the problem is interpreted as a particular type of problem, for instance a communications problem, an internal conflict problem, a technical logistics problem or a marketing research problem. Naming is closely related to framing: relating the problem to an existing frame of reference. Such a frame of reference determines the focus and scope of a project and sets theoretical and empirical boundaries of the problem to be tackled.

This is the first moment during the regulative cycle that the naming and framing process can take place. However, in the following phases of the regulative cycle it should be repeated in more detail. Despite the fact that we will present the naming and framing as a step in the problem-solving process, the link between theory and practice should continually be taken into account.

The problem definition has to be 'managed' throughout the course of the project. Insights gained in the course of the project, or changes in the strategic context of the project, may call for a change in the problem statement. Furthermore, the problem definition may be further refined as more specific performance indicators are chosen in the diagnosis or redesign step. Of course, changes in the problem definition should always be discussed with the principal, as principals are ultimately responsible for the business problems addressed in BPS projects, and therefore have the ultimate say in the problem statement.

5.6 Assignment and deliverables

After the problem has been defined, an assignment can be formulated. The assignment usually consists of a number of sub-assignments. These sub-assignments contain the deliverables of the project, that is, the output generated within the BPS project. These deliverables can be derived from the logic of the regulative cycle. The following deliverables are likely to be relevant for most BPS projects:
- a characterization and validation of the selected business problem;
- an analysis and diagnosis of important causes and consequences of this problem from various relevant perspectives;
- an exploration of potential solutions;
- an elaboration of one of the solutions into a solution design;
- a change plan.

Some students tend to limit the deliverables to the solution. However, all deliverables mentioned have their value for the client. The importance of the change plan will be clear, but already the problem analysis itself may have significant value for the company, as do the alternative potential solutions. These deliverables are used for decision-making on the eventual solution and will be used later if, during or after implementation, changing circumstances necessitate some adaptations to the solution.

Students often finish their BPS project assignments after developing a solution design and change plan. In some projects, additional deliverables may include:
– (supporting) the implementation of the solution design (in a pilot case);
– an evaluation of the implemented solution design.
Notice that the assignment refers to activities that will be executed in the future. The assignment does not state present outcomes of those activities. Therefore, the deliverables in the assignment do not specify, for example, the content of a potential solution.

5.7 Project approach

The next step towards a complete project proposal is the construction of a project approach. The outline of the project is presented in a *conceptual project design*, while an elaboration of the line of work is presented in an *operational project plan*. Of course, it is a plan that may be adapted on the basis of evolving insight. We will first introduce the conceptual project design and then the operational project plan.

For the construction of the conceptual project design, we build upon the ideas of Verschuren and Doorewaard (1999). In a conceptual project design the following elements are addressed:
– the subject of the analysis;
– theoretical perspectives applied in the analysis;
– a confrontation between theoretical perspectives and the subject of analysis;
– the deliverables of the project.
The first element of the conceptual project design is the subject of analysis, that is, the phenomenon that is examined. The subject of analysis is represented in the right-hand box of a conceptual project design (see figure 5.2). In business administration the subject of analysis is usually a business process, a control system, a strategy or a combination of those three. So the subject of the analysis can be (parts of) an operational process, an innovation process, a quality control system, a logistics control system, a financial control system, a marketing strategy, or a technology strategy. Obviously, it is the problem

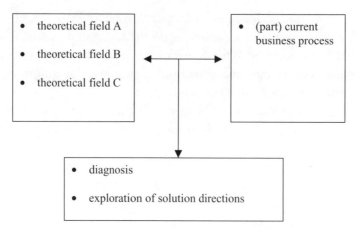

Figure 5.2   General structure of conceptual project design for the diagnosis in BPS projects

selected that determines the subject of analysis. Does the problem concern activities within the operational process? The innovation process? Does it also concern the logistic and/or quality control of the process? Does it concern customer requirements, so that the marketing strategy also has to be taken into account? Once the cause and effect diagram has been made, the subject of the analysis can be determined. Thus, this part of the conceptual project design should be clearly specified.

The second element of the conceptual project design is the set of theoretical perspectives that are required to study the problem. These perspectives are represented on the left-hand side of the model. On the basis of the cause and effect diagram one can list the theoretical fields that are likely to be important during the diagnosis or design phase. Most business administration problems need more than one theoretical discipline to be analyzed or solved. For instance, one may need operations management, information technology, psychology, and change management to understand and solve a production planning problem. In general, practice is too multifaceted to be able to embed it in the ideas of a single theory. Actually, an argument like requisite variety (Ashby 1956) holds that the complexity of the theory or the combination of theories should reflect the complexity of the practical situation. It is an illusion to expect that all relevant theoretical perspectives can be combined into one integrated, homogeneous theory. Theories often focus on different aggregation levels and concern different aspects and objects, which makes them too heterogeneous to integrate. Moreover, they may be applied in different steps of the regulative cycle, as we will see in the next chapters. The set of theoretical perspectives may also include expert opinions about a class

of business problems. These may play a similar role as formal theories. However, the views of organization members should not be included here, because
this second element of the conceptual project design concerns theoretical
perspectives.

Usually, the theoretical perspectives and the current situation of the analysis subject are confronted to come to analysis results and conclusions.
For this confrontation and its implications the following symbol is used:

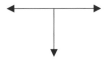

A continuous discussion between theory and practice is required to exploit
the theory-based approach to problem-solving. The confrontation between
theoretical perspectives and the subject of analysis can take several forms. One
form is that theory and practice are compared. The confrontation may also
mean that the current situation is interpreted using theoretical concepts or
evaluated from a theoretical perspective. Chapter 6 will discuss the role of
theory, and therewith the nature of the confrontation, in more detail.

The last element of the conceptual project design, depicted at the bottom
of the model, refers to the deliverables of the project. In general, the conceptual project design presented in the project proposal will be oriented at the
diagnosis – the exploration and validation of the business problem and its
causes – and the exploration of redesign directions. Of course, the diagnosis
and the alternative directions for redesign cannot be specified in advance.
Therefore, the conceptual project design contains a general reference to these
deliverables which will be roughly the same for most projects. We prefer to limit
the conceptual project design in the project proposal to the diagnosis and the
exploration of directions for redesign and to make another conceptual project
design for the later steps of the project. During the course of the diagnosis,
the scope of the project may be limited or extended. Furthermore, redesign
and implementation are likely to require additional theoretical perspectives.
Therefore, it is preferable to draw up another conceptual project design before
the start of the redesign step. If the project also entails an evaluation, that final
step may also require a new conceptual project design.

When the conceptual project design has been constructed, an *operational
project plan* can be developed, based on the conceptual project design. This
project plan is not simply a copy of the conceptual project design. The conceptual design gives the logic of the analysis, the project plan, and how and
when the analysis will actually be carried out. The next step in the process,

the diagnosis, will be more detailed; the project plan is more global for the following steps, since the elaboration of these steps depends on the results of the diagnostic step. Still, the project plan should give a plan up to the final presentation of the deliverables to the client by the student.

The following steps may be part of the project plan:

1. A literature search regarding the topics mentioned in the left-hand side of the conceptual project design. It results in the theoretical ideas and guidelines for the diagnostic step (see also Chapter 11).
2. Empirical analysis of the business problem: investigation of the specific characteristics and the validity of the business problem and the exploration and validation of the cause and consequences of the business problem.
3. Formulation of the diagnosis of the main problem, causes, consequences and their mutual relationships.
4. Exploration of solution directions.
5. Feedback of the results of the former steps to the principal, the company supervisor, and the platform or steering committee (see section 5.8) and the university supervisors.
6. Further detailing of the project plan for solution design and implementation.
7. A further literature search regarding topics on solution design, resulting in among other things design specifications.
8. Elaboration of one direction into a redesign and a change plan.
9. Development of organizational support for the solution and the change plan.
10. Presentation and authorization of the solution and change plan.
11. Implementation (if included in the assignment).
12. Evaluation.

In particular, the second step, the empirical analysis of the business problem, should be described in detail at the start of the analysis step. The main choices regarding analysis activities should be outlined by answering questions such as:

– What is the unit of analysis: departments? Projects? Events? Something else?
– What data will be collected on these units: a qualitative data on a few cases? Comparative data on successful and unsuccessful cases? Quantitative data on a large number of cases? Other types of data? On how many units to collect data? How many for each kind of data?
– What will be the dominant sources of data: interviews? Documents? Computer output?

– How will the analysis be carried out? Is it possible and useful to derive a conceptual model from the literature or will the analysis be inductive in nature? Should we prepare for an evaluation composed of a pre-test and a post-test?

Chapters 6, and 9 to 12, provide guidelines for the execution of the empirical analysis and the use of literature. It is important that the parties involved agree upon the basic design of the empirical analysis, as it determines potential findings, planning and required resources.

5.8 Project costs and organization

The project proposal should also include a section on the costs of the project. There are three different categories of costs. The first category concerns the out-of-pocket costs of the project. This includes a possible trainee allowance and possible travel expenses for the student. The second category concerns resources spent on the project, including the time to be spent by company personnel on interviews, support and supervision (it is important that the company agrees on this) and infrastructural resources (such as an office, or computer support). The third category is a pro memoriam item, and concerns the costs that may be spent to develop and implement the redesign. At this point no one knows what the solution will be, let alone what it will cost. Nevertheless, it should be remembered that this is an issue to be discussed towards the end of the design project.

The project proposal should also contain a section on the organization of the project. The key point here is the choice of principal. This is not necessarily the same person as the initial contact person. The choice of principal is a 'political' decision. The principal must have the authority to decide on the acceptance and implementation of the proposed solution. The implementation of the solution should only, or primarily, change roles and procedures within her or his domain of responsibility. With cross-departmental problems this requirement may result in more than one principal. These people could form a steering committee for the project.

The organization of the project furthermore entails the company daily supervisor and sometimes a project committee or platform if one desires to involve formally key company personnel in the project. A platform is an advisory board, while a steering committee also is involved in the (strategic) decision-making on the project. In general, when the problem is strategically important, a steering group is preferred over a platform. In either a platform or steering group potential conflicting parties may be brought together. Thus, facts and opinions that are found during the project can be shared and checked with all parties, which may lead to a higher degree of shared understanding and inter-subjective agreement. Finally, the university supervisor(s) also form part of the project organization.

5.9 Problem-solving projects in different formats

This handbook has been written largely on the basis of our experiences with BPS projects undertaken by students as graduation projects. Virtually all of these projects are individual ones, carried out as a full-time trainee in a company. For student projects these projects are fairly large as their duration is some six to nine months. Student BPS projects, however, can also be set up to take less time or to be carried out as group projects. The question then is how to adapt project design and management to this different format.

Short individual BPS projects

One can say that the scope of a student BPS project is to be determined on the basis of its length, breadth and depth, that is on its planned duration, the scope of the problem to be tackled, and the depth of analysis and design. If the length or duration of a project is decreased, this should have consequences for breadth and depth. The basic setup of the project, as described in this handbook, may largely be maintained, but the scope of the problem should be adapted to the more limited time available. In our opinion a much more superficial problem analysis and diagnosis is not to be recommended. A good alternative is to agree that students should provide a sound problem analysis and diagnosis and also a number of alternative solutions with advantages and disadvantages of each, but that they are not required to design a detailed solution and change plan. Often this is quite acceptable for the client company and students still get very valuable field experience.

However, if one opts for a short BPS project, for instance with a duration of some six weeks, and possibly not full time, the character of the project has to change. Students will no longer be in-house trainees, but they will do the analysis and design at the university or at their own premises on the basis of a series of company visits. The basic setup of the regulative cycle can still be used, but one will need to limit drastically the scope of the problem to be tackled as well as the depths of analysis and design. For a full BPS project of three months or longer, the didactic objective is to develop the student's skills in real-life BPS. For a shorter project the objective will rather be to get a valuable impression of the opportunities and difficulties of operating in a certain discipline in a real-life environment, unless one opts for a group assignment.

Group BPS projects

If the duration of a BPS project is to be short, there is great potential for a group assignment. As with a short individual project the students will not operate in-house as trainees, but will carry out analysis and design on the basis of data capture by company visits, typically as group visits. A group has much more capacity for analysis and design than an individual, and it has much more potential for depth of analysis and design through the injection of variety and the often intense group discussions. Therefore a group may tackle fairly important problems even in relatively short throughput times of, say, six weeks. The students will not only develop BPS skills but also experience in teamwork which, because of outside pressures, is often much more intense than through team assignments within the university.

The downside is that the project needs much more organizing than an individual one, both externally and internally. Planning group visits to a company for data capture and feedback on results is a non-trivial task. One should try not to plan too many of them. It helps if the principal holds a senior position, so that he or she can ask company personnel to bring some flexibility in their agendas.

Paying attention to the internal organization at the start of the project can avoid a lot of problems. For small teams leadership may be left to emerge, but for teams of five or more members it may be good to appoint a 'project manager'. The project manager is not to act as a 'boss', but has the task of coordinating subtasks, making an overall project plan with clear milestones, monitoring progress, pointing out to the team possible overruns of milestones, and to act as team representative to client and university supervisors. Next to this role the team may want to assign other special roles, like roles with respect to verbal and written reporting, editing the final report or handling the larger calculations.

With respect to content the team may want to create a nearly-decomposable system by breaking down the overall assignment into a number of key issues, and assigning these issues to individuals or to teams of two. As informants typically can be interviewed on more than one issue, the division of tasks in data capture will not always match the division of tasks in analysis and design.

There is also the issue of group dynamics. A group assignment can be an exciting and rewarding experience for students, but it can also be a source of frustration. The group may face problems like free riding, conflict, leadership challenges and disdain for one another's competencies. How to handle such problems, however, falls outside the scope of this handbook.

In order to give an impression of a possible setup of a short group assignment in BPS, and to give an impression of the possible variety of such assignments, we give the fairly specific setup of a group assignment that is used for many years at our school in a two-year postgraduate course programme in designing logistic control systems. The students first do this assignment during the first months of their study, and a second time about a year later. The assignment is to audit the logistics system of a company (or part of a company) and to design the main lines of an improved system. In line with what has been said above, they will not detail their solution, nor design a change plan to implement it. The project is carried out in groups of eight students, four doing it for the first time, four doing it for the second time. Acquisition is done by course management and the intake interview is done by an instructor, accompanied by the student coordinator of the group. Data capture is usually done in no more than two company visits by the group; typically they do some ten interviews. Subsequently problem analysis and design is done in some four weeks (not full time) on the basis of these interviews, using also company data and other written material. For this phase the group is split into two competing teams of four students (the coordinator takes one group, another student becomes the coordinator of the second one). The results are presented to the university supervisors, who decide which team has the best results. The winning team presents the results to the company, and is encouraged to incorporate in their presentation useful elements from the results of the losing team. Students feel that these two field projects are very important learning experiences for them.

5.10 Example

In this section we present an example of a project proposal made for the head of Research Group A, of ABC Research. First, we present summaries of some of the interviews that were held during orientation with stakeholders. Second, we present the project proposal. All required elements are present in this proposal, but for this handbook the text is abridged. Several of the elements receive a more extensive explanation in actual proposals.

When this proposal was made some preliminary work had already been done on the diagnosis of the problem, enabling the student to design

Box 5.3   Examples of parts of four exploratory interviews regarding the ABC Research case

Head of Research Group A

I have worked here for almost two years now. It is striking that no one here knows anything about anyone else. Everyone is in a hurry, is individualistic, and works at home a few days each week. People are only interested in others when they need them with respect to their work. Recently, I had to take over a project that had already been running for two years. Four different people had worked on it and did their part, but no one knew exactly his colleagues' contribution. Moreover, the different parts did not fit together. We need an information system over here with descriptions of former projects and knowledge and skills of the current staff.

Quality manager

The main problem in our department is time pressure. People are in a hurry. They do not meet spontaneously. Senior researchers, who have to coach the younger researchers, prefer to invest in customer contacts, because those can be charged to the customer. Therefore the younger researchers do not get enough supervision. This hurts the quality of their work and hinders their development into competent researchers. This also means that they don't get a clear picture of the knowledge and skills of the senior researchers, so they don't know who to consult on certain issues. This problem has increased following the recent privatization of ABC Research.

Senior researcher

Why is knowledge-sharing among researchers so important? When you really run customer-oriented projects, you will soon find out what the main problems are. We lack sufficient capacity to realize our projects. When capacity is available, it mostly concerns young, inexperienced researchers. We have too few customer contacts within projects. Sometimes, results are not appropriate to current customer needs. These needs may have been changed during the project, but we did not notice. Sometimes we do not know who to consult regarding a particular subject, and probably re-invent the wheel.

Junior researcher

I am very happy to work in this organization. I live quite far away from the office, but I am allowed to work at home as often as I want. Moreover, I can learn a lot from my colleagues. As a junior, I am not required to charge many hours to customers. Actually, there is one problem. When I ask my colleagues very specific questions, they are not very concrete in answering. They seem not to want to share their specialist knowledge, since I may become a competitor for them.

a detailed project approach. In many cases, however, the project proposal is based on a carefully defined problem statement, but without much analysis of its causes. In these cases the designed project approach has a more preliminary nature.

Box 5.4   Example of a project proposal

Project Proposal ABC Research

Problem context

ABC Research, having around 300 employees, is conducting macroeconomic and econometric research for governmental agencies. ABC Research has recently been privatized. It describes its mission as 'being a leader in social science expertise in area X, contributing to the quality of decision-making in policy and business'. This mission creates three challenges: creating value for customers, contributing to scientific development and creating a healthy financial situation. This project focuses on Research Group A, consisting of about 35 researchers. The majority of the projects carried out by these researchers centre on policy evaluation, both *ex post* (measuring effects) and *ex ante* (predicting effects).

Recently, several experienced researchers of Research Group A have left the organization. ABC Research is considered by many as a springboard for a further career. It takes time before new researchers attain the same level of expertise. Due to the privatization, work pressure is high and learning activities tend to be neglected. This poses a threat to the company's mission of being leaders in its field.

Problem definition

Based upon the intake meeting and interviews with members of the ABC Research, the following preliminary cause and effect tree has been developed.

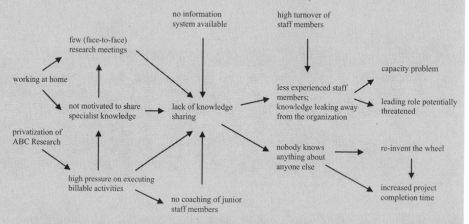

We propose to focus in this project on the following problem:

There is a lack of knowledge sharing among the researchers of Research Group A
Knowledge sharing is not an end in itself and cannot be considered as a performance indicator for the company as such. However, the interviews revealed that the lack of knowledge sharing decreases operational performance (for example project completion time) and threatens the mission of the organization (to be leading in its field). Therefore, this lack of knowledge sharing is proposed as the central problem in this project.

The cause and effect tree presents several potential causes of this problem. Some causes are related to the infrastructure (inadequate IT systems, staff working at home), while others regard project management (lack of capacity), or psychology (individualistic, afraid of sharing specific knowledge) as causes. The cause and effect tree should be interpreted carefully. As it is based on a limited number of interviews, there is no guarantee that the problem and the causes mentioned are valid and reliable, nor that all other important causes have been examined already. However, it indicates some of the directions that will have to be explored.

Assignment

- *Investigate the lack of knowledge sharing within Research Group A*
  First, it has to be determined whether the level of knowledge sharing is actually too low and indeed has the adverse consequences as sketched above. The lack of knowledge sharing was only mentioned in interviews and was not recognized by all interviewees.
- *Determine the actual causes of the lack of knowledge sharing*
  The cause and effect tree presents a number of potential causes. Through theoretical and empirical analysis we need to search for other causes and validate the potential causes.
- *Develop a number of alternative solutions to improve the level of knowledge sharing*
  In order to be able to choose one direction for redesign, the main lines of several alternative solutions have to be designed.
- *Elaborate one alternative solution into a detailed solution and design the accompanying change plan*
  In this project we will develop a redesign that should increase the level of knowledge sharing. We will also design a plan for the implementation of this redesign. However, due to limited time available for this project, the actual implementation of the redesign falls outside the project's scope.

Project approach

Below, we present the *conceptual project design* for the knowledge-sharing problem of ABC Research. This conceptual project design explicates the research subject as well as the theoretical perspectives that will be applied in this project. Later in the project, an adapted conceptual project design will be developed for the redesign phase.

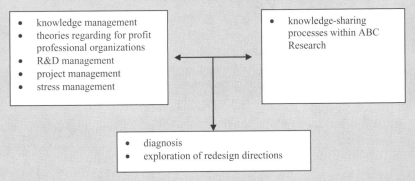

The main theoretical fields required to solve the knowledge-sharing problem at ABC Research follow from the cause and effect diagram. It is clear that the problem concerns knowledge management items in general. But it also concerns the freedom/control dilemma of professionals in a professional organization, and especially within R&D management. Moreover, it concerns the privatization of ABC Research, thus the organization has to make profit, causing competition and time pressure problems. To avoid time pressure problems, good project management is crucial. Applying this kind of reasoning, we come to the left-hand side of the conceptual project design. The focus of this project is on the knowledge-sharing processes within Research Group A. However, knowledge-sharing processes are still a quite unfocused research subject, so it may be focused in the following step of research. Possibilities are a focus on a part of the innovation process and/or a focus on a specific type of knowledge sharing.

The *project plan* is as follows

1. Search for literature on knowledge management in professional organizations and cooperation and coordination within professional organizations. Identify factors that influence interactions between professionals in general and researchers in particular.
2. Analyze the seriousness of the lack of knowledge sharing and determine the causes of this problem and its consequences for ABC Research. Two approaches will be pursued. First, one research project will be analyzed in depth in order to understand the operational process and to identify concrete effects of lacking knowledge sharing. Second, organization members will be asked to identify negative and positive incidents regarding knowledge and these incidents will be used to identify causes.
3. Conclude the diagnosis and discuss with client organization.
4. Develop alternative directions for solutions.
5. Hold a feedback meeting on the diagnosis and proposed alternative solutions. Choice for one redesign direction.
6. Search for literature to support the redesign of knowledge-sharing processes.
7. Elaborate the chosen solution into an object design and realization design.
8. Create support for the object design and realization design.
9. Write the report and make the final presentation.

The planning of the project is roughly as follows. The first four steps will take about four months. Steps 6 to 8 will take another three months. Preparing the final presentation and writing the report will take another month. In total, the project will take eight months from now.

Costs of the project

- An allowance for the master student executing this project.
- Time of staff members for interviews, consultation and supervision.
- To be determined later: costs of the proposed redesign.

Organization of the project

– Principal:	Nick Major (head of Research Group A)
– Company supervisor:	Jack Wolfs (information systems)
– Steering group:	Nick Major, Jack Wolfs, Peter McDonald (quality manager), Steve Goulding, Martin Fuller
– University supervisors:	Hans Berends, Hans van der Bij (University)

6 Theory-based diagnosis of business problems

6.1 Introduction

This chapter concerns the second step of the regulative cycle: the analysis and diagnosis step. Our starting point in this chapter is that the first step, the problem-definition step, has been finished. Thus, in one way or another the problem has been defined, some of its potential causes and consequences identified, the assignment and the problem-solving approach determined.

The purposes of the diagnosis are to validate the business problem, to explore and validate the causes and consequences of the problem, and to develop preliminary ideas about alternative directions to solve the problem. At the end of the diagnostic step students must be convinced and able to convince others of the validity of the problem, its causes and its consequences. During the previous step of the regulative cycle, students are relatively passive. In this diagnostic step the students should be much more active: they must actively develop and execute strategies to explore and check the ideas of the organization members that came up during the definition of the problem.

Students who have little practical experience in business problem-solving (BPS) need more guidelines than more experienced consultants. However, compared with the previous step of problem definition, considerably more activities are situation-specific, which makes it more difficult to provide general guidelines. In our experience, the diagnostic step causes a lot of problems for students. They often do not know how to start and tend to continue the explorative character of the previous step, while part of the analysis strategy should aim at validation, instead of exploration. Thus, valid conclusions must be drawn at the end of the diagnosis and they have to be carefully prepared. The result of the diagnostic step is a problem-oriented or problem- and process-oriented theory on the analysis subject. The explanatory and/or descriptive theory pertains to one case, therefore we will refer to it as an $N = 1$ theory. Since it is a theory, it should meet the quality standards mentioned in Chapter 12.

This chapter is organized around three approaches that should be combined to produce a diagnosis.

First, we focus on *empirical analysis*. An empirical exploration and validation means that the symptoms, their potential causes and their potential consequences have to be identified, and evidence to support the analysis has to be gathered.

Second, we focus upon *theoretical analysis*. Theoretical analysis and empirical analysis should strengthen each other, but there is no standard recipe for doing so. The sequence in which empirical and theoretical analyses alternate, the way in which they interrelate, and the relative emphasis on one or the other differs from project to project.

Third, we focus upon *process-oriented analysis*. Usually a process-oriented analysis supports the analysis of the business problem and its causes. A focus on causes and effects is needed to eventually yield a validation of the business problem and a valid analysis of the causes of that problem. However, if the focus on causes and effects is not accompanied by process-oriented analysis, it may remain rather superficial and detached from actual business practices. In contrast, when there is a focus only on process, it is hard to arrive at an integrated diagnosis.

In section 6.6 we focus on two deviating situations. In some projects, the orientation phase has not resulted in a business problem. In that case the diagnosis has to be preceded by a quick scan. In other projects, the problem is a construction problem instead of a performance-related problem. In those cases, the diagnosis will be limited in nature.

6.2 Empirical exploration and validation of the business problem and its causes

Just like most research projects, design-oriented BPS projects involve a serious amount of empirical analysis. However, the characteristics of data collection and analysis within BPS projects differ from corresponding activities in research projects. In a BPS project it is not a question, hypothesis or theory that is leading, but a business problem. Empirical analysis is needed for: (1) validating that business problem and specifying its characteristics; (2) exploring the causes of the business problem; (3) validating causes of the business problem and determining their relative importance; and (4) mapping the business process. These different aims of empirical study in a BPS project will be discussed subsequently in this section, although they may be executed in parallel or iteratively in an actual project. The mapping of the business process, which supports the exploration and validation of the problem and its causes, and which will be used in the redesign step, will be discussed separately in section 6.4.

Validating the business problem

The first thing that has to be ascertained during the diagnostic step is whether the problem is a real problem, a perception problem or a target problem (Monhemius 1984; see also Chapter 2.1 of this volume). Only when a problem is a real problem is it worthwhile to make it the subject of a BPS project. A *perception problem* reflects a situation where the problem owner has an inaccurate perception of the business system and its performance. For instance, an operations manager may think that the majority of customer complaints refer to bad delivery performance, although defective products are the main ground for complaints. A *target problem* refers to a problem based on unfeasible targets. For instance, the yield of a certain operational process is eighty per cent; this happens to be a common level in the industry, but the operations manager wants to realize a yield of ninety-eight per cent. Problems that are not perception nor target problems are called *real problems*. A real problem refers to a situation that in reality does not meet realistic standards. Therefore, in order to judge whether a problem is a real problem, a perception problem or a target problem, both norms and evidence are needed.

To check the validity of the problem statement, factual information has to be collected. Sometimes it is straightforward to validate the problem. For example, one project focused on the problem that a company often failed to meet service level agreements (SLAs) with regard to a repair service. This company kept track of its monthly scores on SLAs. Using that information, the students could easily verify that only forty per cent of SLAs were met over the previous months, significantly below the company's own standard that eighty per cent should be met. However, in many projects such information is not directly available. Sometimes the required information lies dispersed over documents and databases. In box 6.1 we describe a project in which information that indirectly validated a business problem was collected from invoices and other documents. In other cases it is very difficult to gain factual information to validate the problem. Sometimes one can try to select examples of the problem, stories of situations in which the problem occurred. The least reliable option is to build upon the opinions of organization members as gathered through interviews. Although we strongly encourage students to

Box 6.1   An indirect validation of a business problem

Validating a business problem at a building company

The purchasing manager of a building company worried that the costs associated with the supply process were too high. The purchasing manager asked a group of students to investigate whether cost savings in the supply process were indeed possible. Although the students could not examine directly which costs were unnecessarily high, they could gather factual information on direct antecedents. For four building projects the students gathered information on items that were initially ordered (at the start of the project) from four major suppliers, and information on the items that were actually needed and supplied (and paid for) by those suppliers during the project. In an ideal situation there would be a match between what gets initially ordered and what is actually supplied during the project. By analyzing piles of invoices and other documents the students found that around forty per cent of the initially ordered items did not have to be supplied during the project and was therefore not paid for. The fact that many products that were initially ordered did not have to be supplied, created substantial costs, not only for the purchasing department but especially so for the supplier. Although the costs of these discrepancies were not directly charged to the building company, the suppliers acknowledged that they incorporated these costs in the general price level of the supplied products. These extra costs could not be quantified, nor compared with an exact norm, but for the responsible management the findings verified that there was a cost problem. The next step was to find out what caused the discrepancies.

find other ways to validate the problem, in some cases there is no other source of information available.

To determine whether a performance level is satisfactory or not, the actual performance should be compared with a norm. In the above example the actual SLA score was compared with the company's own norm stating that eighty per cent of SLAs should be met. If in reality such a norm is met, it is a perception problem. If the norm is unattainably high, it is a target problem. Norms can be drawn from several sources. First, they can be stated by the company itself, for example in strategic plans, business objectives or company standards. For example, a logistics service provider with multiple distribution centres determined quality norms for each production centre as the average score of all centres over the last year. Second, norms can also be found by comparing one's own organization with other organizations in the same industry. For several industries such benchmarks are available. Third, scholarly literature may provide the basis for norms.

A validation of a problem usually also means that the problem is further specified. In the example presented in box 6.1 the students were able to identify for which products high costs were likely to be incurred. The more specifically the problem is characterized, the more effectively the causes of the problem can be traced.

Exploration of causes

Once the validity of a problem has been established, its causes can be investigated. If a preliminary cause and effect tree has been constructed for the definition of the business problem, that tree is important input for the diagnosis. However, it is unlikely that the orientation phase has already provided an exhaustive overview of potential causes, which only have to be verified. While executing a BPS project one should also be exploring for additional potential causes. Usually, further exploration also means delving deeper, because the orientation phase often misses *root causes lying behind causes*. So, if it has been established that a particular cause has a significant impact on the problem, the student should explore that cause further.

Qualitative methods, like interviews, are usually most suited for the exploration of causes and effects. Open interviews may take the validated problem as a starting point and directly ask for potential causes. A pitfall of exploration through open interviews, however, is that they keep students in orientation mode for too long. Open interviews sometimes produce rather superficial opinions. The student should try to relate the business problem to the actual operations of the organization. One may proceed by mapping the business process first (see section 6.4). More insight into the business process can also be gained by focusing on specific instances of the process. The student may, for example, explore a specific project or a few production orders. One can also choose to search for specific instances of the problem and explore those, for example by applying the critical incidents approach (see the example of ABC Research below; see also Chapter 10).

Guidance for the exploration can be obtained from theory and from the consideration of potential directions for redesign. Theories may suggest directions in which to search for causes. Theory may also directly suggest potential causes. Through the consideration of potential directions for redesign, the student may also be motivated to explore particular topics further.

The exploration of causes and effects should provide the basis for a fully fledged, integral explanation of the business problem. This integral focus differentiates it from most theory-oriented research. Theory-oriented research usually has a partial focus, shaped by a particular question, hypothesis or model. In a BPS project one cannot be satisfied with information on a limited set of variables. A student should explore as well as possible all factors or variables that could have a significant influence on the performance that has to be improved. This point is reached when new interviews, or new projects or incidents that are considered, do not yield new information. That is, when the empirical analysis is saturated (Glaser and Strauss 1967).

Validation of causes

When potential causes are identified, they need to be validated. Each element and relationship between elements in the cause and effect diagram has to be examined. In order to validate cause and effect relationships, the student should aim at reliable and valid data. Usually this implies a search for 'hard', objective data. We will first present an example in which this was rather easy and afterwards we will turn to some difficulties.

Two students executed a project at a retailer of office supplies, selling exclusively through the Internet. This company faced the problem that too many orders could not be delivered within one day (as the company promised to its customers). One of the potential causes that came up in the orientation was that the picking of the orders in the warehouse took too long. Five potential underlying causes were identified: (1) the warehouse pickers have to walk long distances; (2) the pickers have to search for a long time before they find the required products; (3) the pickers have to wait for a long time before they receive orders from administration; (4) the pickers spend a lot of time processing backorders; (5) the pickers lose a lot of time due to out-of-stocks. The students checked each of these branches of this part of the cause and effect tree. For 140 orders they measured how much time was spent on each of these five activities. They found out that these five potential causes took respectively nine, twelve, thirty-eight, three and eight per cent of time (the other thirty per cent was spent on actually picking the products and miscellaneous activities). These percentages were compared with standard figures found in literature. They concluded that the third potential cause – waiting to receive orders from administration – was the most important cause of long picking times compared with both other factors and the standard figures.

A typical problem experienced in student BPS projects is lack of information. Much of the information that they would like to have is not readily available. In that case, students depend upon their own creativity and their own data-collection initiatives. If they are lucky, the information can be gathered from existing sources. If there are no documents or databases that

Box 6.2   Multiple sources of evidence

Multiple sources of evidence

A BPS project at a car manufacturer focused on production breakdowns due to a lack of spare parts. The student executing this project studied the impact of this cause in three ways. First, interviews were held with mechanics and operators. These people estimated that in five per cent of cases a breakdown was caused by a lack of spare parts. Second, 581 downtime notifications were examined. In eleven per cent of cases the spare parts that were needed were not available. Third, the actual stock levels of spare parts were observed. From these stock levels it was estimated that the likelihood that a required spare part being out of stock was four per cent. This student concluded that in at least four per cent of cases a lack of spare parts caused a production breakdown.

hold the relevant information, students can also choose to create quantifiable information themselves, for example through observation (like in the warehouse example above) or through a survey.

Validation of causes can also occur through qualitative data collection and analysis. If an appropriate unit of analysis is chosen (for example orders, projects, or incidents) and data are analyzed systematically, qualitative analysis may also provide justifiable conclusions. It is also possible to let people within the client organization judge whether or not something is a cause of the business problem. In order to claim some level of reliability, the student should aim for some inter-subjective agreement (the relevant beliefs should be shared by at least two different people, preferably from two different departments).

Box 6.2 presents an example in which three different sources of information for the same issue were used, as an incentive to think creatively about possible sources of information.

Even when it is clear that a particular state of affairs conforms to expectations, it is not always clear whether it really is a cause. Stated in theoretical terms: it is hard to determine the internal validity of proposed relationships. In the example on order picking times, a direct causal relationship exists between the potential causes and the problem that had to be explained. More time spent on an activity automatically means an increase in total time spent on picking orders. However, causal relationships are often more ambiguous. For example, in the ABC Research case, one of the potential causes was that researchers frequently work at home. As such, the amount of time spent working at home can easily be validated. However, it is not immediately clear to what extent that may have a detrimental effect on knowledge sharing.

Finally, the relative importance of the causes or lines of causes must be determined. In the warehouse example, the effects of the potential causes could be neatly compared, because they were measured in the same way. Frequently, it is more difficult to compare the strength of the impact of different causes. It is much harder to compare, for example, the effects of working at home, lack of motivation, and the inadequate IT system on the amount of knowledge sharing. One option to do so is to build upon the judgment of members of the different groups that are involved in the problem. An efficient way of executing such research is by using the members of the platform or steering committee. This step is required, since not all causes are equally important to the problem selected, and it is too much work to try to solve each cause. Of course, the selection of the most important causes should be done very carefully; otherwise all the work that has been done already becomes worthless.

While this section has discussed the use of empirical analysis in the diagnosis of a BPS project, Chapter 10 will present a more elaborate discussion of qualitative methods for data collection and analysis. We strongly recommend reading that chapter in addition to this one when planning a diagnostic study. Furthermore, if quantitative methods are to be used, we refer the student to more specific handbooks on operations research and social science research methods.

6.3 Theoretical analysis

A diagnosis should be based on both empirical analysis and theoretical analysis. In the previous section we described the empirical analysis of a business problem and its causes without referring to theory. However, empirical analysis and theoretical analysis should go hand in hand with each other. In this section we discuss how theory, and scholarly literature in general, can contribute to a diagnosis. Yet, the relative emphasis on theory or empirical data may differ from project to project as well as the way theory and data are interrelated. In this section we describe a number of ways in which theory can be used, ranging from a dominance of empirical analysis to a dominance of theory.

It should be noted that theory can never be the sole source of a diagnosis. Theory is by definition general (or mid-range). To make theoretical ideas publishable, researchers have to distance themselves from the complexity of practice. Therefore, theory always has to be contextualized for use in actual BPS. Students are required to use theory creatively and to combine multiple perspectives.

Literature as support

A 'light' way to use existing literature is as an extra source of *evidence* on causal relationships. Causes or lines of causes are validated when they are mentioned in reliable literature. This is especially valuable when it can be established that two particular factors are present but when at the same time it cannot be claimed on empirical grounds that these factors are causally related. When such a causal relationship has already been established in the literature, this can serve as evidence for a causal relationship in this particular case (as long as this particular case matches the context in which the empirical study tested this relationship).

Conceptualization

Theoretical literature can also provide the *concepts* to interpret empirical phenomena. The preliminary cause and effect tree is likely to contain many non-theoretical factors. Translating these non-theoretical factors into theoretical concepts often helps to sharpen the analysis. By subsuming bottlenecks under more abstract theoretical concepts, a cause and effect tree can become more structured. Furthermore, conceptualizing bottlenecks and causes in theoretical terms helps to build more firmly on existing literature.

The conceptualization of causes and effects requires creativity on the part of the student. We encourage students to play with different theories, to interpret the problem in the light of different theories, in order to discover the perspectives that illuminate the problem.

The timing of this conceptualization is important. If it is done late in the diagnosis, the theoretical perspectives cannot guide data collection any more. If it is done early in the diagnosis, it may be unclear what perspectives will be useful.

Although theory may be explicitly used to conceptualize causes and effects, it is often used more implicitly. Students who are educated in business administration are likely to use basic concepts without recognizing them as theoretical concepts. Examples are 'lead time', 'organization structure', 'marketing strategy', and 'knowledge sharing'. Moreover, organization members also use theoretical concepts, acquired through education, organizational socialization, and reading professional literature. On the one hand this helps in the conceptualization of the business problem. On the other hand, it may be a threat as it may exclude other interpretations of the same underlying empirical phenomena.

Suggesting causes

Existing literature may also suggest alternative causes. As one of the dependent variables in an article is related to the selected business problem, the independent variables may reflect causes of the business problem. To select the literature and the new causes, it is important to know that the literature is reliable and valid for the practical situation. How these two conditions can be checked is explained in detail in Chapters 11 and 12. Besides the formal requirements on reliability and validity, the context studied in the articles selected should correspond with the practical situation in the BPS project.

Theory as a guiding framework

For some business problems a comprehensive theoretical framework is available in the literature. The overarching theoretical framework may be a *causal model*, covering the main problem, and a line of reasoning embedding several causes of the cause and effect diagram. In that case the next step is to measure the dependent and independent variables of the framework, using the scales that have been developed for these variables. In general, the empirical problem will be reflected in the current value of the dependent variable. If that is the case, students can try to explain the empirical problem in terms of the combination of current values of independent variables. Of course, the theoretical framework must be valid for the practical setting.

The overarching theoretical framework may also be a description of a *solution concept*, or a system or process. In that case the current business process or system may be compared with the literature, after which specific attention should be paid to deviances from the theoretical framework. However, there are less of those types of frameworks available in the literature than some managers and students assume. Moreover, even presumably exhaustive models only cover limited aspects of most problems.

It is advisable to explore alternative explanations, based upon alternative frameworks or on the basis of the preliminary cause and effect diagram. We recommend elaborating at least one of these alternative explanations. In the end, one must select the most likely explanation, or combine both explanations, and complete the diagnostic story (see section 6.5).

Example of ABC Research

The following paragraphs provide an example of the combination of empirical and theoretical analysis. This example concerns a project at ABC Research, for which a project proposal was presented in Chapter 5. Within this proposal the organizational problem was named and framed as a knowledge management problem, consisting of a lack of knowledge sharing among the ABC researchers. A characteristic for this project is that the student started with an empirical analysis and then used theory to interpret findings and to facilitate the transition to the redesign step.

The empirical analysis has been executed along two lines of research. First, a typical research project was examined thoroughly in order to get acquainted with the work done at ABC Research. The examination of the research project was important to understand the research activities that were executed in the project teams of ABC Research (this is a light version of a process analysis; see Chapter 10.4). Second, a critical incident analysis was conducted (see Chapter 10). Both lines strengthened each other and were intended to check whether the problem was a real problem and to empirically explore and validate the preliminary cause and effect diagram.

In the critical incident analysis nineteen incidents were examined, based on twelve interviews with six ABC researchers. The student conducted two interviews with each respondent. He started by presenting two examples of typical incidents regarding knowledge sharing in order to trigger respondents. In the first interview a list of potential incidents was developed. During the second interview, interesting incidents were selected, and a cause and effect diagram was constructed for each incident selected. The fact that each ABC researcher was able to recount several knowledge sharing incidents was interpreted as a validation of the existence of a knowledge sharing problem.

After the analysis of individual incidents, a cross-cause analysis was executed. Using the grounded theory approach (see Chapter 10), all causes of all incidents were structured into homogeneous categories. The student selected the most important categories, that is the categories with most causes (a cause counted for two when mentioned in two incidents). The result of the analysis was the identification of four interrelated categories of causes: environmental pressure, lean project structure, lack of overview of expertise, and the existence of isolated subgroups (see figure 6.1).

After this empirical exploration the student, the principal and the supervisors decided to focus primarily on the lean project structure. The work in projects was divided in work packages which had to be integrated near the end of the project. However, during the course of the project little formal and informal communication was organized between the researchers executing the work packages, causing incidents in several projects. Additionally, the student focused on the existence of isolated subgroups within ABC Research.

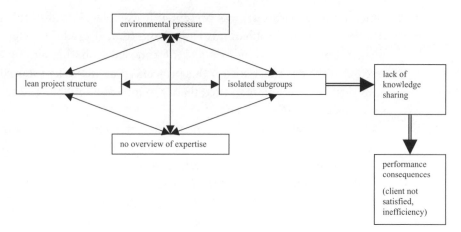

Figure 6.1 Results of incident analysis at ABC Research

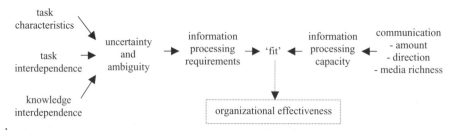

Figure 6.2 Information processing model (adapted from Tushman 1978 and Daft and Lengel 1986)

He did not take the environmental pressure (for example the high number of billable days required) further into account as that cause fell outside of the problem owner's scope of responsibility. Furthermore the lack of overview of expertise was not considered during the remainder of the project because a 'yellow pages' system was already in development to tackle that issue.

In a subsequent *theoretical analysis* the causes relating to the lean project structure were *conceptualized* using the information processing approach, as presented by Tushman and Nadler (1978) and elaborated by Daft and Lengel (1986). The information processing approach claims that organizations should match information processing capacities and their antecedents with information processing requirements and their antecedents. This basic line of reasoning is represented in figure 6.2.

The incidents showed that the actual processing of information and knowledge did not always match the information processing requirements within projects. Additional analysis of the incidents revealed that these information processing requirements stemmed from strong interdependencies between subtasks in some of the projects. In the lean project structure, these task inter-dependencies were not adequately dealt with. Furthermore, several incidents were due to the neglect of knowledge interdependencies, meaning that employees needed the specialized knowledge of colleagues to execute their task in the right way (Faraj and Sproull 2000). Therefore, the student added the concept of knowledge interdependence to the information processing model. He concluded that the degrees of task and knowledge interdependence differed from project to project and that the communication structure was insufficient in projects with strong interdependencies.

According to the incident analysis, the lean project structure and the existence of isolated subgroups mutually reinforced each other. Therefore, the student constructed an alternative theoretical interpretation of the problem focusing on group psychological aspects. He used the model of Cohen and Bailey (1997) on team performance, which emphasizes organizational behaviour attributes like social norms and conflicts that may have detrimental effects on project team performance. At ABC Research, differences in social norms and conflicts were indeed observed between the isolated subgroups. The student concluded that in fact both the information processing framework and the group psychological interpretation reflected important parts of the current situation. However, he decided to put more emphasis on the transformation of the current communication structure, since he found that a lot of conflicts originated from a lack of communication, while the lacking communication increased the differences in social norms between different sections that were already present.

In this project the conceptualization of the empirical findings in theoretical terms facilitated the transition toward the design of a solution, because the information processing approach implies a set of design guidelines. The basis for the student's redesign was to make a distinction between projects with high and low degrees of interdependence and to design different communication structures, varying in intensity and media richness, for these types of projects. Project leaders were assigned a central role in realising the match between interdependencies and the communication structures within their projects.

6.4 Process-oriented analysis

In order to explore and validate causes and effects it is often useful to combine a focus on the business process with a focus on the cause and effect tree. If one focuses strongly on the cause and effect tree, one runs the risk of staying away from the actual business processes and therewith producing a rather superficial analysis. Students also have to analyze thoroughly the business process early in the diagnosis. The idea of the process-oriented approach is that first a general description of this business process is developed, including both the operational process and the control system and also including performance norm. A theoretical underpinning of this distinction between a cause and effect approach and a process-oriented approach can be found in Mohr's (1982) distinction between variance theories and process theories.

A limited use of a process-oriented approach is to analyze the business process in order to gain a background understanding of it. In the ABC Research example, the student started the diagnosis phase by analyzing one research project that was recently finished. This enabled him to understand the work processes of the researchers and served as a background to study incidents from a wide range of projects. When only the latter approach was taken, it was less likely that this student would have been able to relate observations of knowledge sharing to actual business practices and operational performance.

Some projects require an elaborate description of business processes. A more detailed description of the business process can be obtained by conducting about fifteen to twenty semi-structured interviews with respondents from different disciplines pertaining to the research subject, by observation, and/or by studying documents (for example the quality manual). For each discipline at least two respondents are required in order to reach a reliable result. A starting point for the data collection can be the platform or steering committee. Note that documents describing the desired situation in the company may not reflect the actual situation precisely; a check is required in that case.

A completely unstructured situation will seldom occur in a manufacturing setting, but it may occur in an innovation department or a consultancy firm. When processes are unstructured, one may take projects or orders as units of analysis and execute a cross-case analysis using the grounded theory approach. The grounded theory approach is a structured way to develop local theory from scratch on the basis of empirical data from interviews, document analysis, or observation (see Chapter 10.5). For a further understanding of processes one may also use process theory (see for example Van de Ven and Poole 1995).

In order to obtain a higher level of reliability of the description of the research subject, a check on the whole description can be conducted by the platform or steering committee (if present). Once the business process in question has been described, a more problem-oriented approach is required

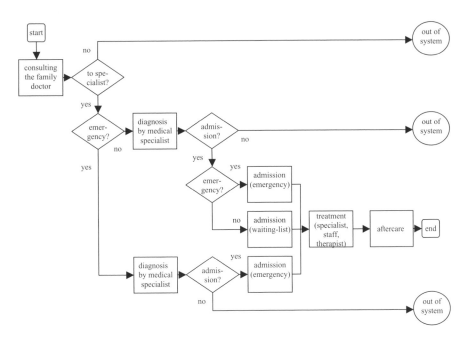

Figure 6.3   An example of a process diagram (Gerards 1998)

by an efficient quick scan (if necessary), and an efficient exploration and validation of the cause and effect diagram.

There are a great number of ways to describe processes and the way these are controlled. One can, for instance, use the five simple symbols for respectively operation, decision, terminal, flow line and connector, given by ANSI (the American National Standards Institute; see *The Certified Quality Manager Handbook*, 1999, Chapter 38) for an example. Another possibility, mostly used for information processing, is the set of integrated definition (IDEF) methods (which can be downloaded from www.idef.com).

We will illustrate the role of process analysis by means of an example of a project carried out at a regional hospital. The student who executed this project started her diagnosis by charting the primary process concerning patients suffering from chronic obstructive pulmonary diseases (COPD). She interviewed representatives of all stakeholders of the process: medical specialists, nurses, planners, staff of the emergency department, social workers, and laboratory staff members. Based on these interviews she constructed process diagrams using the ANSI symbols. The highest level diagram is presented in figure 6.3, showing five activities undertaken within this healthcare process: consulting the family doctor, diagnoses by the medical specialist, admission, treatment

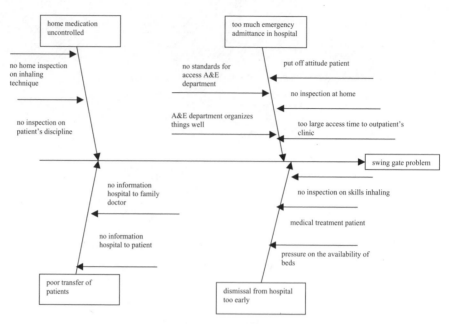

Figure 6.4   Ishikawa diagram for a group of patients with chronic obstructive pulmonary diseases (Gerards 1998)

and aftercare. For each of these activities a more detailed process diagram was constructed, containing information on throughput time, responsibilities and decision criteria. She returned to her respondents with additional questions that came up while constructing these diagrams. Furthermore, she discussed preliminary diagrams with the respondents, in order to check her interpretations and increase the reliability of the process analysis.

This process analysis served as the background for the investigation of bottlenecks within the process. The orientation phase of this project did not yet result in a clear problem statement. Further empirical analysis was conducted by means of investigating incidents within process steps and at the interfaces of activities. This incident analysis yielded a central problem: too many patients returned with similar health problems, and it revealed causes of this problem. These causes were represented in an Ishikawa diagram (see Figure 6.4). The following section discusses the resulting diagnosis.

6.5 The diagnostic story

Once the most important (lines of) causes have been selected, the diagnostic story can be developed. This is a one-liner summarizing the main points of the diagnosis. Below, we will give the example of a story of the diagnosis from the project on COPD patients in a regional hospital (which was introduced in the previous section).

The problem, called in this project the swing gate problem, concerns the perception of hospital staff that patients return to the hospital too soon after their dismissal. The main causes for this are mentioned in the Ishikawa diagram of figure 6.4: dismissal from the hospital too early, poor transfer of information to patients and family doctor, a lack of inspection at home as to whether medication (by inhaling) has been taken and whether the inhalation is done in the right way, and too much emergency admittance in the hospital. However, the listing of the main causes does not give much insight in the interrelationship of the causes and the relationship with the problem. Therefore, a diagnostic story is required. It is based on two corner stones, on the one hand the fact that patients are dismissed without thorough training in the inhaling technique and an inspection of whether the technique is applied correctly, and on the other the fact that patients are not informed about the development of their disease. Because of the lack of training in inhalation at home, the inhalation goes wrong, resulting in a quick deterioration of the disease. Because of a lack of information about the development of the disease, the patients do not know when they have to return to the hospital. Therefore they take action too late, and an emergency admittance is required. This increases the pressure on the available beds, resulting in a dismissal of patients without thorough training on inhaling. In this way, the swing gate problem gets worse and is never solved.

6.6 Alternative approaches

An extended diagnosis: quick scan

A quick scan may be applied when there is not an appropriate cause and effect diagram at the beginning of the diagnostic step. To build a preliminary diagram, some steps from the problem-definition stage can be executed.

However, sometimes there is not even a rough sketch of a problem or problematic topic. In that case we prefer a thorough analysis of the organization. The first step is to identify performance problems that can be observed or are perceived from outside of the organization. Performance problems may include quality problems, flexibility problems, cost problems, or availability problems. As we have mentioned before, from the perspective of business engineering we often focus on the operational level for identifying problems. Performance indicators on which the scores are below standard, or below the expectation of clients or managers should be selected. The next step is to identify a business system for which the performance and the causes of poor performance can be studied. Then an internal exploration can be executed with an emphasis on the indicator(s) below standard, or below expectation. The final step is to analyze the findings, to structure them into a cause and effect diagram, and to select a problem. After the quick scan, one can proceed with the exploration and validation of the cause and effect diagram.

The need of a quick scan does not always reflect a failure of the first step of the regulative cycle (definition of the problem). It may also mean that the problem selected during the first step of the regulative cycle is not defined on an appropriate aggregation level to diagnose and solve it. An example of the latter can be found in the company where a student was confronted with a knowledge sharing problem at the level of the innovation division. However, the problem itself could only be analyzed and solved at the level of innovation projects. Thus, knowledge sharing had to be studied and improved within and between projects. Therefore a prerequisite of the study was that people on the project level also experienced knowledge sharing problems. In that case the cause and effect diagram had to be rebuilt for the project level.

A limited diagnosis: a design-oriented approach

In some cases the client organization defines a problem in terms of a desired object or system, not available in the present situation. If that is not a perception problem, there is no need for a diagnosis, but only of a further analysis and justification of the need for that object or system. In such cases the problem may be formulated in terms of a clear, but not yet satisfied need, like when there is a need for a physical infrastructure to make Internet connections, or there is a need for a warehouse. In such situations one can proceed after the analysis of the need with the next step of the regulative cycle. In this case we may call it the design step, instead of the redesign step, since a completely new object or system has to be constructed.

In this approach one may follow the descriptive part of the process-oriented approach. Anyway, either during the diagnostic step, or in the design step, a lot of descriptive information about the current situation is required to make the design match the current circumstances. For instance, the physical infrastructure should enable Internet connections that are compatible with the current, local information systems with respect to availability, speed, safety etc. When the information gathering about current circumstances is postponed to the design step, this step will take considerably more time than when a full diagnosis is executed.

A limited diagnosis may also include an analysis of the history of the problem involved. It is important to know whether earlier attempts at solving the problem have been undertaken and why these attempts, if any, were unsuccessful. This may yield insight in factors and forces that have to be surmounted or circumvented in the design and implementation steps.

Note that a justification of the need is important. Sometimes on further consideration the need proves to be less obvious. For instance at ABC Research, at the start of the project the principal wanted us just to design a 'yellow pages' IT-system, containing references to experts on several topics. Although it appeared as a main cause (actually a category) in our diagnosis, we were quite convinced that such a reference system would not be used at ABC Research on a large scale, so long as the isolated subgroups existed. So, a more thorough diagnosis regarding other main causes, and their interrelationships, as well as relevant directions for a redesign, was required at ABC Research, and we were able to convince the principal that this was necessary.

6.7 Final remarks

The diagnostic step turns out to be a difficult phase in the regulative cycle. In our experience the result of this step is often too poor to proceed with the next step. When the so-called diagnostic story, in terms of interrelated main factors that will cause and enlarge the problem selected, cannot be told, the diagnosis is still not clear enough. An example of a poor diagnostic story is a list of business problems that are not interrelated, and not described in terms of causes, symptoms, and consequences. In that case the development of a coherent redesign is very difficult. One can only try to solve each problem separately, and that will lead to an incoherent set of solutions. The only way to solve the problem of a poor diagnosis is to spend more time interrelating problems and causes with each other, and structuring the list of problems into a coherent diagram of causes, symptoms, and consequences. Another problem that may occur is a lack of broad organizational support for the diagnosis. Regular contacts with the various stakeholders can prevent or solve this problem.

Another threat is that students continue the diagnostic phase for too long, believing erroneously that a redesign will follow automatically from a diagnosis when they have enough information. As a result, they keep on searching for information and analyzing problems from different perspectives. As will be discussed in the next chapter, designing a solution involves a creative leap. In order to facilitate the transition to the design phase and to sharpen the diagnosis, it is often valuable to explore redesign directions while being engaged in the diagnostic step. When engaged in the redesign step, there will often be the need and the opportunity to return to a diagnostic mode for further data collection and analysis on specific issues.

7 Solution design

7.1 Introduction

In the regulative cycle, the 'analysis and diagnosis' step is followed by the 'plan of action' step, which involves solution design (discussed in this chapter) and change plan design (addressed in the next chapter). For the student, solution design is often the most difficult part, even if the problem statement and the diagnosis step give a firm starting point. For various reasons there are far fewer systematic approaches available in the literature for design than for analysis. Nevertheless the present chapter will give some ideas for solution design, and the next one will give some ideas for the design of the change process, to be used for the realization of the solution.

7.2 The deliverables of the business problem-solving project

A business problem-solving (BPS) project is only complete when the designed solution has been realized and the intended performance improvement has been achieved (at least to a satisfactory degree). The ultimate deliverable of the project is the intended performance improvement of the business system in question.

If problem-solvers are part of the business system to be changed (in a managerial or professional role), they will usually participate in the change process and support the quest for performance improvement. However, if the project is a consultancy project for a student, it is usually agreed that the student will not participate in the change and realization phase. In that case the deliverables of the project are (as stated in chapter 2.1) the following:
- a problem definition;
- a problem analysis and a diagnosis of the major causes and consequences of the problem;

- an exploration of potential solutions for the problem;
- an elaboration of one of them in a detailed solution design and a change plan;
- a more immaterial deliverable, of organizational support for the solution and change plan.

The first four deliverables can be regarded as 'knowledge products'. The last one is rather a 'social product', the result of interactions between the student and the various stakeholders during analysis and design.

Of course, the deliverables of the project have to be agreed upon during the intake of the project and the orientation. In particular it should be clear at the project start to what extent the student is to be involved in the actual change process after the design of the solution and accompanying change plan and their acceptance by the client organization.

The basic idea on which the BPS project is based holds that the successful realization of the designed solution should result in the solution of the defined business problem. That solution is a model of the new business system (new structure and/or work process) or of a new tool or procedure supporting the business system, together with its internal and external interfaces.

A redesign of a business process may involve a change in the sequence of process steps, eliminating some steps, integrating new ones, redesigning a whole step, or designing tools to support certain process steps. A redesigned business process may be in the form of a flow chart with text, explaining among other things the tasks and responsibilities of the various actors in the process. Or the redesign may concern the organization structure of a certain part of the company, integrating some positions or departments or allocating some tasks to different positions, or changing the mission of a department. In that case the form of the redesign may be an organization chart with explanatory text.

In some cases the problem may be solved with fairly limited intervention or redesign. In that case one might want to refrain from making a complete model of the new situation. However, the solution design should give some insight into the relationship of the intervention with its business system environment.

7.3 The design process

The basic cognitive activities in a BPS project are analysis and design. These two activities are quite different in character. In analysis the dominant logic is from question to answer, in design it is rather from solution to specifications.

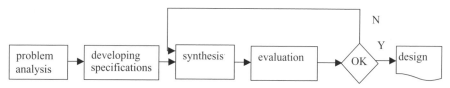

Figure 7.1   The key activities in actual designing: synthesis-evaluation iterations

Usually it is quite possible to proceed logically from a question on how things are, to an answer via a predefined route of analytical steps: on the basis of a research question one makes a research design and the execution of the research process on the basis of that design should, and often does, produce the answer.

Typically a question has one good answer. On the other hand, a design problem, the question of how things should be, is open-ended; usually more than one good design is possible. If one asks three architects to design a building on the basis of the same set of specifications, one gets three, often very different, designs. This is one of the reasons that it is usually not possible to predefine a route from problem to solution. One starts with the problem, followed by problem analysis, diagnosis of the causes of the problem, and definition of the specifications to which the solution should conform, all still fairly logical. But then comes a *creative leap* towards a possible solution. The previous activities may have produced some hints for possible solutions, but they certainly do not control the creative leap. After this leap logic comes in again through the comparison of the expected behaviour and performance of the proposed business system in the immaterial domain of designing ('on paper', as discussed in chapter 3.5) with the specifications, of which the most important one is, of course, that the solution should solve the problem. So in designing the core logic it is not from question to answer, but from solution to problem, that is logically evaluating whether the solution solves the problem.

As said in chapter 3.5, the key activities in actual designing are synthesis-evaluation iterations (see figure 7.1). The synthesis is the creative leap, the evaluation the subsequent rational and logical comparison of the solution with the specifications. On the creative leap itself not much can be said, but careful management of the inputs to the synthesis step can strongly support it (see section 7.4). Furthermore, there is quite a lot of literature on creativity and the management of creativity (see for example Ackoff and Vergara (1981) and Hicks (1995).

One way of developing creative solutions to business problems is *idealized design* (Ackoff 1981b). In idealized design one designs an 'ideal' solution to the business problem. It must be a viable solution from technical, economical and social viewpoints, so it certainly should be no science fiction. But it should be ideal in the sense that one does not take into account the problems of changing the present to the ideal, as one often does in business system redesign. So, idealized design is intentionally not a redesign. Once the ideal design has been made, one investigates to what extent it may be implemented, this time taking into account the problems of changing the present system. In 'normal' design the solution is approached from the present situation, in idealized design from the ideal.

In the evaluation step the expected performance of the redesigned business system or the contribution of the new tool to the business system is assessed. As discussed in chapter 3.6, business systems are socio-technical systems. If the technical component is dominant, as can be the case in inventory control or shop-floor scheduling, it can be possible to make a mathematical model of the designed system. In that case the expected performance of the new system can be assessed by mathematical calculations or simulation. If, however, the social component is dominant, mathematical modelling will not give much insight. In that case evaluation is better done on the basis of *case-based reasoning* (see for example Leake 1996; Watson 1997; Bergman *et al* 1999). To evaluate the performance of a not-yet realized system, one searches for similar, already realized and well-documented cases, and predicts the performance of the new object on the basis of a comparison with other cases. In BPS projects the present situation is one of the cases used for comparison: one analyses the differences between the present and the redesigned system and tries, usually in a dialogue with people familiar with the present system, to assess what the impact of the changes can be. Unlike senior management consultants, students typically will not have similar cases at their disposal, but company personnel may have. Of course both academic and management literature can be a rich source of similar cases.

To illustrate these vital synthesis-analysis iterations we will discuss a design issue from the International Imaging Systems (IIS) case, presented in section 7.6 and chapter 8.4. The student had to design the input to a decision-making process with respect to starting and discontinuing research and design projects. One of these inputs was an overview of the present portfolio of projects. So she had to decide what information to include for each project. She started by making a list of parameters to include on the basis of her present knowledge of the situation (synthesis). She then turned to the literature study she had made earlier to see whether important parameters were omitted (evaluation) and added four more (synthesis). She discussed this with the company project planner (evaluation) and found that for two of them no reliable information could be provided. But after consultation with the administration she concluded that for one of them acceptable approximations could be made and that the other must be skipped (synthesis). Then she compared the resulting list with specifications (evaluation), in other words she assessed whether the information given was indeed sufficient to support rational decision-making, and she discussed this with the two principals of the project. They agreed with her that this was sufficient information, after which work on the design issue was discontinued for the time being. Of course it was always possible that further design on other issues would lead to new insights, necessitating new work on this one.

7.4 Solution design

There is not much to say about the synthesis, the creative leap towards possible solutions. However, there is much more to say about the input to this step. There are three types of input:
- *problem related inputs*: the problem definition, the problem analysis and diagnosis (see Chapters 5 and 6), and the specifications, that is the requirements the solution has to fulfil;
- *a model of the present business system* as a starting point for the redesign;
- *ideas for possible solutions*.
The problem related inputs provide the starting point for the design process. Without sound problem related inputs the design process operates on quick sand. When students threaten to go under during the design process, they often succeed to find firm ground again by returning to the problem statement and diagnosis (re-reading the problem statement and diagnosis can be enough, but one might also find that these need further sharpening). As discussed above, these problem related inputs are needed for the evaluations steps during the design phase, but they are also important for the eventual justification of the designed solution.

Typically a solution to a business problem is a *redesign* of an existing system or tool. If it is a redesign, the starting point is a model of the present business system. Even if one wants to use idealized design, as discussed, one needs this model of the present situation in order to know what it is one has to design. The choices of the level of detail and the boundaries of that model are important design decisions, as elements and aspects of reality that are not included in that model will remain 'invisible' during the redesign process and hence will also tend to remain hidden in the model of the new business system. The model of the present business system should be complete, incorporating both the problematic elements to be changed and the sound elements to be retained. Finally, it often is a requirement for the redesign to change as little as possible.

Ideas for possible solutions are the final type of inputs to the design process. The first important source of ideas is the diagnosis of the causes of the business problem. That diagnosis can provide clues for solution design. However, that solution cannot be logically deduced from the diagnosis. The diagnosis is about what is, the solution about what can be.

A second important source of ideas is, of course, the client organization. Usually the problem has been around for some time and various stakeholders may have ideas on possible solutions. The project may even have been started to detail and implement a solution that has already been more or less accepted. Using ideas from the client organization can have cognitive advantages, but can also have advantages from the point of view of change management: involving the client organization in a redesign may substantially reduce resistance to the realization of the redesign. However, there are also dangers: a particular solution may promote the interests of some stakeholders, but harm those of others. By using ideas from some stakeholders the student may get involved in difficult organizational politics. The use of ideas from the client organization may also cause the student to share the local 'tunnel vision'. Involving an outsider in business problem-solving should also provide an opportunity for injection of fresh, new ideas. So one should be wary of using internal ideas in BPS.

For sound BPS the literature is a third source of ideas. In fact both the scholarly and the management literature provide a wealth of solution concepts (see chapter 4.2), and general ideas on how to plan and organize business activities of all kinds. Examples of solution concepts for organization structures are the functional structure, the business-unit structure, the matrix structure, the front office-back office structure and so on. Or, solution concepts for the layout of a shop floor are process layout, product layout, cellular layout and fixed position layout.

Solution concepts have a general nature. So students have to do two things. First they must choose which solution concept (or which combination of solution concepts) would be best suited as a basis for solution design, and second, they must redesign the solution concept from the general to the specific, making a specific solution for their specific business problem.

Ideas are, of course, an important input to the synthesis of solutions. Therefore students should put substantial effort into making an inventory of ideas on possible solutions. They should do this right from the start of the project as, especially during the initial phases, when one is still unhampered by knowledge and prejudices with respect to the problem, one tends to be very open to and creative in generating new ideas.

The actual design follows synthesis-evaluation iterations: possible solutions are evaluated against the specifications. Using the design theory from chapter 3.5, such specifications may include the following:
– functional requirements;
  • realization of the solution should solve the business problem, which is the key requirement;
  • the benefits should exceed the costs;
– user requirements:
  • the people presently working in the business system (or using the present tools or procedures) should have the competences needed to work in the new system or to use the new tools or procedures (so realization may involve some training);
  • the new system should be user-friendly;
– boundary conditions:
  • the system should comply with legal requirements, including those on health and safety;
  • the system should comply with the present business policies of the company (unless the objective of the project is to change such policies);
  • the system should fit with the present company culture (unless, again, the objective of the project is to change some basic ideas on, for example, how to deal with customers or with subordinates);
– design restrictions:
  • the project should take no more than X months;
  • no more than Y euros should be spent;
  • the realization of the solution should change as little as possible in the present business system.

Many of these specifications are fairly obvious. Nevertheless, in the heat of the project execution they can be overlooked, which can lead to problems for the justification of the solution (some requirements may pop up only at that moment) or in the realization. The set of four types of specifications may also serve as a kind of checklist for students to elicit specifications from their client system.

7.5 Solution justification

Finally, there is the key issue of the justification of the designed solution at the end of the design process. Justification uses the results of the evaluation steps, but evaluation is done from the perspective of the student, needed in order to make design decisions. Justification is done vis-à-vis the client organization in order to enable the client to decide whether or not to implement the designed solution. In a sound approach one uses a 'no surprises' policy, in other words the student has previously discussed the design (or a preliminary design, or elements of the design, see the illustration in section 7.3) with various stakeholders. On the one hand this is to test the quality of the design and to get an idea of the possible resistance to it, and on the other hand it is to enable the client system to become acquainted with the designed solution, and possibly to create some sense of ownership within the client organization with respect to it. Nevertheless, at the end of the design step the designed solution is subjected to some formal go no go decision-making by the principal (who will often rely on recommendations from other stakeholders) and at that point the student should be able to formally justify the design.

Following chapter 3.7, justification should be done on the basis of:
– a description of the process of analysis and design that has produced the solution;
– an explanation of why the student is of the opinion that realization of the solution will solve the problem;
– a cost/benefit analysis, both operational and financial (as far as possible).
The first element of the justification should give the client an insight into the quality of the analysis and design process, just like in an academic publication truth claims are justified on the basis of the research process that produced the research results. An important part of this is a description of the inputs to the design process (see section 7.4).

The cornerstone of the justification is the explanation by the student why he/she judges that the implementation of the solution will solve the problem. A solution justification needs a sound problem statement and diagnosis. This is always the case but especially so if the new business system has a predominant social component. In that case, as discussed in section 7.3, evaluation is based on qualitative reasoning rather than on calculations or simulations on the basis of a mathematical model. Such reasoning needs to start from the firm ground of a sound problem analysis and diagnosis.

Solution justification is essential, but in the real world of business it is not a process to create certainties. Principals are used to being presented with approximations, and a sound approach to problem-solving implies that one gives the principal a fair picture of the risks and uncertainties of the follow-up process. One must give an account of the reasons why the benefits of the solution will exceed the costs, at the same time being clear about the possible limitations of the justification. Typically it is difficult to formally *prove* that the solution will solve the problem.

Students must also give a cost-benefit analysis, because even if the solution solves the problem, it may be too costly, and not justifiable by the benefits of solving the problem. This cost/benefit analysis refers to the costs of real-ization and subsequent operation of the new system and the benefits of the improved performance. It does not refer to the costs of the problem-solving project itself up to this point; these are sunk costs which can no longer be influenced. Like the justification with respect to the solving of the problem, this cost/benefit analysis can also be difficult to make. Typically the costs can be reasonably estimated, both in operational and in monetary terms, but an estimate of the monetary benefits may be difficult to calculate. How-ever, in many cases, a justification in terms of operational improvements may be quite acceptable to the client as managers are used to deciding on cer-tain expenditures for certain operational advantages. For instance, a rough cost/benefit analysis at the end of the design phase of a BPS project in the field of new product development may be as follows. The proposed solution (a new stage-gate system for managing new produced development) will decrease the throughput time of an average development project from twelve to some nine months, the implementation process will take some four months and will cost some seven man weeks from the staff people assigned to that implementa-tion process. Operational costs of the new system will be some four per cent higher than present costs (plus, of course, a justification of the figures given above).

The final version of the designed solution should be presented together with an accompanying change plan. Change plan design is part of the design step after the problem analysis. However, for didactical reasons change planning will be discussed in the next chapter, together with a discussion of the change process itself.

7.6 Solution design: the International Imaging Systems Case

International Imaging Systems (IIS) is a small company specialising in digital TV cameras for medical applications (in x-ray equipment), military applications (air reconnaissance) and for various industrial applications. It is situated in The Netherlands and employs some forty-five people. Although small, it is world market leader in its medical niche and a strong player in its other markets. Its research and development (R&D) resources are very limited, but by focusing on a few core competences, it arrives at developing technologically cutting-edge products. Its customers are mostly large, sophisticated companies. Its product ideas are to a large extent generated by these customers or by the innovative suppliers of their key components, in particular the sensor chip of the camera.

The company is organized in three main departments: marketing and sales (eight people), R&D (sixteen people) and operations (twenty-eight people), plus some central staff, including a few people in administration and human resources management.

Business problem

IIS is very successful in terms of profit and growth. Its main problems, however, are its limited range of competences and especially its very limited R&D resources. The BPS project was initiated because the two owner/directors of ISS, the principals of the assignment, felt that they did not use their R&D resources optimally. Clearly this was a strategic issue for the company, even if it was less clear how much room for improvement there was. They asked one of our students to design for her graduation project some kind of portfolio management system for IIS.

Problem analysis and diagnosis

Although the principals had clear ideas on the type of solution they wanted, the student started, in line with sound problem-solving principles, with problem analysis and diagnosis, not only to generate information for solution design, but also to check the problem itself and whether the proposed type of solution would indeed solve the problem. She also needed a good description of the present process of decision-making on new projects as input for her redesign. In the formal assignment the possible sub-optimal utilization of the present

R&D resources was defined as the problem, and more formal management of the portfolio of product development project was mentioned as a possible solution. The assignment left open the possibility that problem analysis and diagnosis would also lead to other types of solutions.

The problem analysis showed that there was indeed ample room for improvement. Among other things there were too many development projects running at the same time, defocusing development efforts. Project deadlines were often unrealistic (and not met) because of a lack of insight in available capacity, and short-term incremental projects tended to drive out more radical, strategic innovation projects, which are vital for the long-term continuity of the company. The diagnosis was that the present way of decision-making on starting or stopping development projects was an important cause of this state of affairs. This decision-making was somewhat haphazard, more based on short-term commercial opportunities than on strategy, and based on incomplete information (such as insufficient knowledge of available capacity and of the consequences of reallocating capacity as a new project was launched). The conclusion was that a more formalized system for managing the portfolio of product development projects might solve the problem.

Solution design

The student used for her solution design the various inputs, mentioned in section 7.4. Problem-related inputs were important, that is the problem definition and problem analysis, the model of the present system and the specifications for the new system of portfolio management. These were not very specific. She discussed briefly with the two principals the general specifications, mentioned in section 7.4. Both agreed that these applied to this design as well and they didn't come up with specific new ones. But they did stress the user requirements: as IIS is a small, informal company, they did want to stick to simple procedures. They wanted a robust portfolio management system, not one that was too sophisticated. On the other hand, present business polices were not much of a boundary condition. There were not many of them in the first place and both principals were quite prepared to change policies where necessary.

In the course of the problem analysis the student produced a thorough description of the existing methods of decision-making on development projects. She did not develop a formal, mathematical model but devised a process scheme of the various steps the company usually followed, and included explanatory text and a discussion of the kind of deviations from this procedure that occurred from time to time. This description had been used for problem analysis, but it was also an input to the redesign of the system. The client organization provided ideas for solutions, including the principals' idea to formalize portfolio management, along with ideas on various detailed design problems such as how to describe the present portfolio of projects (see below). As an extra the student also carried out some brief benchmarking studies on portfolio management in three other companies to get ideas on real-life portfolio management systems. (In the event she did not get many new ideas from these studies, but she did get a feeling for the feasibility of such systems in practice).

The project was also theory-based. Early in the project the student undertook a literature study on product development management in general and on portfolio management in particular. This provided her with many ideas on how to assess the present system and on how design a better portfolio management system.

Good design is playing with alternatives. In this case the student did not design more than one overall alternative, but she did play with alternatives for certain design parameters such as the degree of formalization (the application of the principle of minimal specification: what elements to include in the formal system, and what elements to leave to judgment and improvisation).

As said in section 7.3, synthesis-evaluation iterations form the core of the design process. In this case the evaluation of the various design options was not done on a mathematical basis or through simulation, but purely through judgement on the basis of case-based reasoning, using the literature, three benchmarking studies, and the experience of company informants. The student compared her solutions with the literature and she used the collective experience of her client organization to judge the feasibility and expected outcomes of the various solutions.

This is not to say that her solution design went smoothly from specifications to an accepted design. Her first design proved to be far too sophisticated for the client company, so she had to simplify it. She also had difficulties with the financial aspects of her system. Admonished by the literature, she wanted to give discounted cash flow calculations for each new development project. However, it proved too difficult to get reliable figures on future sales, especially for the more important, breakthrough projects. Eventually she dropped these calculations and used in the prioritizing of a project an indicator for its expected impact on sales, ranging from one to five and based on a consensus, reached at the review meeting (in this company there were no big differences in gross margins between the various products, so impact on sales was also a good indicator for profitability). See also the illustration in section 7.3 on the synthesis-evaluation iterations to get a further idea of the vagaries of business system designing.

The designed solution

As required, her designed portfolio management system was simple and robust. It followed the basic idea that you first design a process, then work out how you want to control it, what information is needed, and then organize it, that is design the various roles in the process and assign these roles to actors or departments. The student used the idea that you first control a process and, once it is under control, you start to optimize it.

The student designed a decision-making process consisting of a regular portfolio review meeting supported by an information system. Key design parameters included the frequency of the meetings (it started as a monthly meeting), the business functions to be represented in these meetings, and their roles in preparing the meeting, in decision-making and in the follow-up. A central role was the secretarial one, responsible for the information system, for preparing the meeting and for producing the minutes. The idea was to assign this role to the present project planner.

At the core of the system she designed a simple computer-supported information system, giving in each run a list of present and proposed development projects with key parameters and a list of capacity groups with information on their actual and proposed use. Initially, before optimizing, the parameters per project included objectives, required capacity from the various capacity groups (in this case respectively systems engineering, electrical engineering, mechanical engineering and software engineering), and the names of the engineers providing that capacity, the present status of the project and the planned completion date. The information per capacity group included time-phased total available capacity, time-phased allocated capacity (plus the projects using that capacity), and time-phased requested capacity for proposed projects. Because of the simplicity of the system, she did not choose to use a standard project management software package, but she did need to design (and implement) a standard way of describing the progress of development projects in a number of phases. (Prior to this management had authorized the start of a project, whereupon it entered a kind of 'tunnel' – the development process – after which the project only came in sight again after leaving that tunnel at completion, or if failure had to be reported. In the new system management also got information on progress through the tunnel). She also designed standard categories for projects, like platform projects, additions to product families, derivative products and product maintenance projects (for example to solve customer complaints).

Review meetings and the information system made the situation controllable: the information system calculated the consequences of the addition or deletion of projects and of the reallocation of resources, so decisions could be made with a clear view of the consequences of the various alternatives, and these decisions could be implemented and monitored clearly. Subsequent optimization rested heavily on the prioritizing of projects. IIS had recently implemented (a fairly informal but effective) system of technology road mapping, which provided the company with a sound basis for defining technology strategy. Our student also developed a simple set of criteria indicating the relative importance of each project (among other things based on the typology, mentioned above, on expected impact on sales, and on the potential for future derivative products). The technology strategy, this grading of importance, and the key project parameters from the information system, were all inputs to the actual decision-making at the review meeting (in which, of course, the two directors played the main role).

Justification

The student justified her solution partly on the basis of a description of the process that had produced that solution. This description showed that she did indeed use a broad array of inputs, both from the literature and from various people within the company, to analyze the problem and to design the solution. The description also showed that she utilized the experience of company people and her university supervisors to evaluate her system.

The cornerstone of her justification was a discussion of why she felt that this solution would solve the problem. The discussion was strongly based on the problem analysis and her own evaluation of her solution described above. She made it plausible that her more formalized and stronger fact-based decision-making, using a robust system of prioritizing, would create conditions for a better use of development resources. (Note that she did not promise actual better use, as this would strongly depend on how the company – and especially the two directors – would use her system; see also Chapter 8.4 on this issue).

She also produced a cost/benefit analysis: the costs in terms of time and money to run the system (the development costs were already paid for via her graduation project), and the benefits, not in monetary terms but in terms of an improved use of development resources.

In addition one may remark that in business not only the credibility of the message counts, but also the credibility of the messenger. The student had made her analyses and designs not in an ivory tower, but in good contact with key company personnel. This gave them a sense of ownership of the project and its solution, thereby enhancing its credibility.

8 Change plan design and the actual change process

8.1 The timing of change plan design

At the time of formal go-no/go decision making on the designed solution, one should also make decisions on the change process itself. That decision-making should be based on a change plan, specifying the various actions to be taken, the actors that are to execute those actions, and the actors that should get involved in the process. Decision-making on realization concerns the authorization of the change plan (after possible amendments) and the assignment of people to the planned actions by the managers responsible (normally according to the proposals in the change plan).

The change plan should be made before the formal go-no/go decision-making. In fact, change planning should start right at the beginning of the project. Every business problem is embedded in a political-cultural environment, of which the student forms a part. The mere fact that the student enters the organization to work on a certain problem already has an impact, among other things because it increases the awareness and perceived importance of the problem in question. Quite early in the project the student should make a *potential stakeholder analysis*: which people are expected to be the *direct stakeholders*, that is, people whose work processes, roles or vital interests are directly affected by the problem or by possible solutions, and which people are the *indirect stakeholders*, that is, the people who are to cooperate with the direct stakeholders and therefore need to know about the problem and about the changes in roles and processes of the direct stakeholders. Students plan their series of interviews on the basis of this initial stakeholder analysis. These interviews are not only to produce technical-economic information on the problem and possible solutions, but also to involve the stakeholders (to some extent) in the problem-solving process.

More specific change planning should start at the same time as the exploration of possible solutions to the business problem. This is, among other things, to get an impression of the costs of change and the possible resistance to the solution in question: knowledge on costs and resistance may influence the choice of solution. A definitive change plan can only be made after it is known *what* is to be changed, but an outline change plan can be designed after the outline design of the solution has been made. Further detailing can then be done in parallel with the detailing of that outline design. In any case, if change planning is only started after the solution design has been finalized, it is usually too late. In that case the student has missed the opportunity to interact with the client organization on the designed solution and the change plan, resulting in possible flaws in the designed solution and not enough insight into the costs of and resistance to change. (See section 8.5 for an illustration of the problems students can run into if they are too late in giving attention to organizational change issues.)

In this handbook we try to limit our use of the term 'implementation' because this term suggests that the solution is an immutable entity to be 'inserted' into a passive organization. Rather the designed solution, the redesigned business system, is *an important starting point and guide for the subsequent change process and the process of learning for performance.* The designed solution is not immutable, but is adapted through the second redesign, discussed in Chapter 3.6, to requirements at the individual level and possibly also to some extent to personal ideas and preferences. During the change process the solution may also be adapted to changed circumstances as the organization and its environment will not stand still during 'implementation'.

8.2 Change plan design

'Organizational change is a context-dependent, unpredictable, non-linear process, in which intended strategies often lead to unintended outcomes.' (Balogun and Johnson 2005, p 1573). We agree that all planned organizational change is difficult to manage, but this does not mean that such processes are unmanageable. Furthermore, Balogun and Johnson's statement applies to particularly large-scale change processes, that of frame-breaking changes affecting large organizations. Change processes on a smaller scale are far easier to manage.

Change processes, resulting from student business problem-solving (BPS) projects, are seldom on a large scale, but they can still involve significant organizational change for the client organization. In this chapter we discuss the change plan for such a significant change. For planned changes on a smaller scale (such as in the example in section 8.4) a similar approach can be used, although the planned interventions tend to be simpler, as the example will show.

The contents of a change plan are the following:

– a specification of the redesigned business system and its intended performance, the *objectives* of the change process, plus a so-called '*delta-analysis*', that is an analysis of the major differences between the present business system and the redesigned one; the change interventions should focus on these major changes;
– a specification of the *actions* to be taken to realize the planned changes, plus their timing;
– a specification of the *people* who have to execute these actions and of the people who have to get involved in the change process;
– a design of the *change organization,* that is the temporary structure within which the above-mentioned people will work;
– a *communications plan*, specifying the ways and the timing of informing the various stakeholder groups on the nature, timing and progress of the change plan.

The actions to be taken may include further detailing of the designed solution. They may also include the purchasing of equipment or software, or the realization of changes in the physical infrastructure of the organization.

The choice of people who are to carry out the change plan takes into account the various kinds of expertise needed for realization. It may also be pertinent to create a certain representation in the change organization of the departments most affected by the proposed change. An important decision is to what extent one should use outside people if internal capacity or expertise is lacking, or if it is appropriate to use people without any personal interest in the change in order to defuse possible political problems.

With respect to the change organization, it may be relevant to create one or more *working groups* to detail the solution and to prepare the change. If there are several working groups, there should also be a coordinating *project team* to link the various working groups. If the change affects several departments, there could be a steering committee consisting of the managers of these departments (preferably not their representatives, in order have a steering committee with real decision-making powers).

Finally, the most important critical success factor for realization is having a sound communication plan. People active in the change organization themselves tend to underestimate the information gap between themselves and the rest of the organization. Lack of information is a potent source of resistance, producing not only uncertainty but often also mistrust.

The actual design of a change plan can be quite straightforward, provided there is sound background analysis on which to prepare it. This background analysis starts with the above-mentioned delta-analysis. The focus should be on the major changes. Unless technically very complex, the minor changes can usually be looked after by the people within the business system, provided they have a thorough understanding of the new system (note the importance of the communication plan here), and provided they are sufficiently motivated to cooperate.

On the basis of these major changes, a final stakeholder analysis is made, followed by an analysis of the resistance to the proposed changes for each (group of) stakeholder(s). This analysis of resistance to change can use the checklist below (see Van Aken 2002; see also for example Chin and Benne 1976; and Kotter 1978). For each individual direct stakeholder, or for each group of direct stakeholders, one or more of the following sources of resistance may be present:

- *lack of understanding*: people may not understand that there is a problem (so they are not prepared to put an effort into the change process), or they do not understand the new system, or they may misunderstand the consequences of the change for their own position and work processes;
- *differences in opinion*: people may understand the problem but disagree with the solution for technical, economic or personal reasons;
- *lack of trust*: in the members of the change organization, either in their *intentions* ('they say they want to split our department because they want more focus, but in reality they eventually want to close down our part of it') or in their *competences* ('the idea of export to Eastern Europe is a sound one, but they really have no idea what that involves, so it will be a failure');
- *low willingness to change*: direct stakeholders may not want to change because they fear the unknown, or fear that they will not perform well in the new system, or just don't want to lose a familiar organizational environment. There may be an *inherent low willingness to change*, possibly related to the history of the organization or department (for example because of a recent mismanaged change process), or related to the type of people (for example having a low employability and hence fearing change). Or there may be an *induced low willingness to change*, caused by an unprofessional approach to the change process: at first they are quite willing to cooperate but they lose that willingness because of ill-advised actions by the change agents.

Over-specification of the design, for example incorporating too many details in the designed formal system, can also lead to induced low willingness to change, because the people concerned may experience the new system as a kind of straightjacket;

– *conflicts of interest*: organizational changes tend not to be neutral with respect to the material or immaterial interests of the various stakeholders; some may win, others may loose. An important category of changes causing conflicts of interests are changes involving redundancies or transfers to other departments.

An analysis of resistance to change needs some empathy: students should try to understand what the proposed change really means for the various direct stakeholders. This is difficult; people in the change organization tend to underestimate the impact of a change on the stakeholders. One may also ask people what they think of the proposed change, although one should remain critical with the answers. People may not want to say what they really think because they fear that it may harm their position in the new business system. Resistance caused by conflict of interest tends to be expressed in terms of differences in opinion, based on technical or economic arguments rather than political ones, which are rather taboo in many organizations.

The analysis of the resistance to this particular change is the basis for the design of the *intervention strategy*. This design of the intervention strategy builds on Tichy's TPC-model (Tichy 1983), already mentioned in chapter 3.2. According to Tichy, one should manage organizational change processes simultaneously in three intertwined aspect systems (intertwined like the strands of a rope):

– the *technical system* (T), the domain of technical and economic issues, like the business problem itself and its strategic context, and the new business system that should solve the problem;

– the *political system* (P), the domain of material and immaterial interests and of the formal and informal power individuals and groups may use to protect these interests;

– the *cultural system* (C), the domain of corporate and departmental culture, of corporate, group and individual identity, and of the emotions connected with the close and repetitive interactions with other people within the organization.

In each system there are various interventions to deal with the issues in that system. The typical *technical intervention* is the report, spelling out what the business problem is, why it is important to do something about it, what solution has been designed, and why that solution will solve the problem.

The typical *political intervention* is the formal order. Something like 'yes, we understand your objections to the solution, we may even agree with some of them, but in the interests of the company as a whole we will proceed with the proposed solution, so, please, do as you are told'. Appointments and dismissals are an important type of formal order. People opposing the change may be dismissed or transferred and their successors appointed with the mission of making a success of the planned change.

The *typical cultural intervention* is participation. This involves including (potential) stakeholders in the definition and analysis of the problem, in the design of the solution, and in the design of the change process. Participation can contribute to the (technical) quality of the new system, can foster the understanding of it, and can produce a sense of ownership.

A given, specific intervention may fall in one of these three main categories. However, in practice an intervention often is a kind of hybrid, falling in two or all three categories. For example, if the CEO of a company gives a presentation to company personnel on the business problem and its proposed solution, this intervention may have the character of all three. The technical content of the presentation is a technical intervention; the fact that the CEO (and not a consultant or staff officer) gives the presentation is a political one (making it difficult for the audience to oppose the change openly); and if the CEO extends a credible invitation to think along with him/her to solve the problem or to detail the solution, the presentation can also be seen as a cultural intervention, intended to produce participation.

An *intervention strategy* is an outline plan of steps to be taken, along with a mix of interventions to be used in the change process: can we confine our interventions to technical ones, by explaining the change to the various stakeholders, or do we also need strong political and/or cultural interventions? It depends on the expected resistance. If the main source of resistance is a lack of understanding, technical interventions in the form of further explanations of the problem and the proposed solution, would be sufficient. If the main source of resistance is differences of opinion, a combination of technical and political interventions would be appropriate: technical discussions followed by possible amendments to the solution and a political intervention to decide on the remaining issues.

If the main source of resistance is a lack of trust in intentions, cultural interventions would help if that mistrust is unfounded (if mistrust is justified, such an intervention is, of course, dangerous). If there is a lack of trust in competences, again cultural interventions may help if the mistrust is unfounded. If there are good reasons for a lack of trust in competences, one may want to put other people in charge of the change process.

If the main source of resistance is a low willingness to change, again cultural interventions may be used – next to technical ones – as this may help people to get more familiar with the problem and its solution and may relieve some of the fears connected with the change.

If, finally, the main source of resistance is conflicts of interests, one may need to use political interventions.

In case of a pure design approach to the change process, see Chapter 3.3, the series of steps in the change strategy can, for example, simply be:

– a formal announcement to the organization;
– a subsequent detailing of the plans per department or group;
– a preparation phase (in which the necessary appointments are made if they haven't been already);
– the formal start of the new organization structure or business system;
– a planned period of learning;
– a formal evaluation and planning of final adaptations on a given date.

However, one may also use a change strategy with elements of a developing approach by using a pilot implementation. As discussed in Chapter 3.3, one may want to use this approach if there is insufficient design knowledge to predict the performance of the new business system 'on paper'. In that case one can learn from a real-life pilot implementation and design the definitive system on the basis of what has been learned in the pilot.

Delta analysis, analysis of resistance and the design of an intervention strategy, prepare the way for the actual design of the change plan, the contents of which have been discussed above.

The functional requirements for the change plan include the demand that its execution results in the realization of the designed solution. User requirements and boundary conditions are quite similar to the ones for the solution design discussed in Chapter 7.4, and the main design restriction is usually a limitation in throughput time and costs.

8.3 The change process

The change process is managed on the basis of the designed solution and the change plan. The solution defines the business system to be realized and the change plan defines how that is to be done. Like the design of the analysis and design process discussed in Chapter 3.5, the change plan specifies *the undisturbed process*, how that process will unfold if all goes according to plan. As it rarely goes exactly to plan, the people in the change organization (project leader, team leaders and others) have to adapt the realization actions to changing circumstances.

Usually any deviations from the plan are at the change and realization stage more often than at the analysis and design stage. Often the latter activities can largely be shielded from interferences from day-to-day operations. A good project plan, sound agreements on the time to be spent on analysis and design, and a management convinced of the importance of the project, can see to that. But changes in organization and work processes interact necessarily with daily operations. However important the change, these daily operations are the lifeline of the organization, so prioritization is difficult and the never-ending problems in daily operations impact on the change process. (Because of this, some say that an organizational change process is like changing the tires of a moving car.) For this reason in Chapter 2.1 we used the term 'change muddle' to characterize the change process. Still, a sound change plan can permit process management to get a grip on the change process and to manage it on a kind of management-by-exception basis. But one has to be flexible and have the capacity to improvise.

Change processes start with a phase in which the formal changes are prepared and introduced. During this phase the change process gets much attention from management and other people in the business system. After that phase has ended, usually by a formal start on a certain day of the new system, a phase of learning-for-performance starts (see Chapter 2.1). This phase can be quite protracted, which can lead to a certain loss of management attention and to an incomplete realization of the planned improvement in business results. Therefore it is a good idea to incorporate in the change plan, a formal evaluation of the change and its results towards the end of the change process to see what has been accomplished and what still has to be done.

As mentioned in Chapters 5.6 and 7.2, the deliverables of a student BPS project include not only the solution and the accompanying change plan, but also the problem statement, problem analysis and diagnosis, and the exploration of alternative solutions. A major function of these latter deliverables is to support the possible necessary adaptations during this learning phase. If things develop differently from expectations, one can return to the problem and the alternative solutions and assess whether the solution is still valid, which adaptations might still produce the intended results, and which are to be avoided.

8.4 Change plan design: the International Imaging Systems case

In Chapter 7.6 we discussed the design of a solution to the problem of the sub-optimal allocation of product development resources of International Imaging Systems (IIS). Now we will discuss the design of the change plan for this solution.

Preparing the change process

In the very early stages of the BPS project the student made a potential stakeholder analysis: who were expected to be the direct stakeholders, whose work or vital interests were directly affected by the problem or by possible solutions, and who were the indirect stakeholders, whose cooperation patterns might change because of changes in work processes.

The student identified as direct stakeholders the two owner-directors, the three managers of the research and development, marketing and sales, and operations departments, the project planner and other members of the research and development department. The other people in the marketing and sales department, the quality manager, and the controller were regarded as indirect stakeholders. The student decided that during analysis and design she would give special attention to the two directors, the research and development manager and especially the project planner. (It was expected that the latter would have to play an important role in the new setup of portfolio management and, furthermore, he might resent the idea that a university student had been asked to redesign 'his' system.) All direct and indirect stakeholders were informed at the start of the BPS project on its objectives and setup, either directly by the directors or through their department manager. Halfway through the project the student informed all stakeholders (many of them in individual meetings) on the intermediate results of her project. Other meetings were arranged during the analysis and design process where it was deemed useful.

The meetings with the stakeholders were initially to share with them the defined business problem in order to prepare for change, and to get information on the problem and ideas for solutions (also on prior attempts to solve the problem, which can be very illuminating; however in this case the awareness of the problem had only just emerged). In later stages the objective of these meetings was to test intermediate results, both with respect to technical content and possible resistance to possible solutions. In this project the development of ideas went fairly smoothly, but the project planner proved indeed to be a hard nut to crack. However, after some time the student did get him involved in her project and towards the end he largely agreed with her proposals. The full support she enjoyed from the two directors was a great help in this. In the direction of the project planner this worked more or less as a political intervention.

Designing the change strategy

Before designing the actual change plan, the student designed a change strategy on the basis of an analysis of the possible resistance to the new portfolio management system. Such an analysis typically is a 'back office' activity, to be shared with university supervisors and colleagues, but in principle not with the client as resistance to change can be a sensitive subject.

The student started with a 'delta analysis', specifying the key elements of the proposed change. This included more formalized decision-making on research and development project starts and stops, and more formalized feedback to management on their progress. Using the checklist of section 8.2 she came to the following assessment of the resistance to change:

- *lack of understanding*: because of the intense communication with the four key direct stakeholders, the student did not expect any lack of understanding with them. But it certainly was important to give the other stakeholders ample information on the new system once it had been authorized;
- *differences in opinion*: towards the end of the project there were no significant differences of opinion with respect to her proposals, as far as she could judge on the basis of her contacts. However it was clear that some only gave her the benefit of the doubt: 'it looks all very well on paper; let's hope it will work in practice';
- *lack of trust*: the student shared the problem with all stakeholders early in the project; nobody had reason to distrust her intentions or those of her principals. Neither did her handling of the project give people reason to question her competences. A certain lack of trust in competences was present in the sense that some doubted whether the two directors would be prepared to fully use a system that might constrain their discretion in decision-making, or that they would show sufficient perseverance to keep the system going after a possibly promising start (see also the doubts expressed at 'differences of opinion');
- *low willingness of change*: this was certainly present with the project planner at the start of the project, but because of cultural interventions (the student's

persistence in getting him involved in the project), it was almost gone towards the end of the project. The main issue then was to what extent the two directors were willing to change their decision-making behaviour. The student had also used cultural interventions with respect to the two directors by way of detailed communication on the new system, and they repeatedly expressed their willingness to co-operate, but she felt that this issue could still threaten the success of her system;

– *conflicts of interest*: this might have been the case if someone other than the present project planner was given the role of secretary to the portfolio review meeting. As this was not the case, there were no conflicts of interests. Furthermore, the improved monitoring of project progress in the new system could have been threatening for the development engineers, but communication with them showed that they expected this to be more than compensated for by a better focusing of their efforts (less projects at the same time) and more realistic deadlines. Another point might have been a (limited) shift in the power balance between the two directors and the three department managers as the new system 'gave voice' to them during decision-making, voices that were not heard in the old days of haphazard decision-making in face-to-face meetings between the two directors. However, the relationships between the various actors in the company were such that this was not to be expected.

In summary, perseverance in new decision-making behaviour by the two directors seemed to be the main issue in resistance to change (provided, of course, that the various stakeholders would be informed well on the new system after final authorization).

This resulted in the following steps:

– the student discussed the above-mentioned issue – in somewhat guarded terms – with the two directors (they recognized the problem and promised 'to behave');
– she organized two pilot sessions of the portfolio review meeting in order for the directors to experience the more formal decision-making procedure;
– and she made a change plan.

Change plan

The change plan is a formal document to be authorized at the same time as the designed solution. It is to be used by company personnel, together with the documentation of the new system, after the design part of the BPS project is complete, after the student has left.

The change plan contained the following elements:
- the objectives of the change process, the realization of an improved utilization of product development resources and a better realization of (more realistic) deadlines;
- a description of the main changes, in this case setting up a formal portfolio management system consisting of a regular review meeting supported by a secretary and an information system;
- the actions to be taken after the formal authorization of the system and change plan. In this case these were fairly simple as the change had already been well prepared. The new system and change plan were to be authorized in a formal meeting in which the student would give a final presentation of them. At this meeting the two directors should be present, as well as the three department heads, the project planner, the controller, and the quality manager (and also the two university supervisors). This meant that after that meeting all key personnel would be well-informed. Formal training in the new system was not necessary because of the two pilot runs. (But further learning and adaptation was indeed expected but not planned). Therefore the planned actions were merely:
  • informing stakeholders (see below);
  • planning the first series of 'real' review meetings by the project planner;
  • formally assigning the project planner to plan and prepare these review meetings;
  • agreeing on a date (in fact the date of one of the future review meetings) on which a formal evaluation of the system would be made and possible improvements planned, and assigning to the project planner the task of preparing that evaluation.
  This also meant that the change would not be managed as a formal project, that no project organization would be setup, and no external personnel would be hired to support the change process;
- Because key stakeholders were already informed before and at the authorization meeting, the communication plan merely consisted of the following steps:
  • a brief memo would be written by the student describing the new system and justifying its introduction;
  • the research and development manager would convene a meeting for members of his and the marketing department, including the marketing and sales manager, to explain the new system and then distribute the memo to the audience.

Through the authorization meeting and this follow-up meeting it was felt that all stakeholders would be sufficiently informed.

As we have seen, in this case the change plan was fairly simple, as the change itself was not very radical and the change process was well-prepared by the interactive way in which the student had done her analysis and design.

8.5 Change plan design: the importance of developing organizational support

For students a BPS project is an exercise to develop their competences in applying (management) theory in practice. Therefore students have to focus on the content of the problem. However they should also pay attention to process, paying special attention to change planning and developing organizational support for their solution. As an illustration, we describe below a project from the early days of the development of our methodology that went less well than the IIS project.

It concerned a relatively small business unit of a multinational electronics firm in the field of large weighing systems, for instance for weighing trucks. It was a design to order operation, orders ranging from €100,000 to €5 million. Although the competitive pressures were not very high, the profit level of the business unit was disappointing. Management decided that major causes were high cost levels due to the great variety of the projects, and the use of too many custom-built modules. Standardization of modules would greatly help to reduce costs. A student from our course program was asked to develop a so-called 'configurator'. This is a software tool that supports the quotations made by the sales engineers to prospective customers. On the basis of the performance requirements stated by the customer and a database of technical data, the tool was to propose a combination of standard modules which would satisfy the given requirements. By thus reducing the number of custom-built modules costs should be decreased significantly. On the basis of data from the development department and interviews with development engineers, the student developed a tool that was able to produce good proposals for system configurations, and technically it seemed to be a very successful project.

However, when presented to the sales engineers, all hell broke lose. The system was in their view unworkable, the proposals generated by the system unacceptable for the customer, and the possible cost reductions minimal because many custom modules would still be needed. Management, at first happy with the system, became confused by the plethora of technical and commercial arguments and eventually scuttled the project. So the project proved to be a failure. (However, the supervisors produced a good academic publication on the project, with the student as co-author, as technically it was an interesting solution.)

In hindsight one can easily see that the project failed because of a number of reasons. The student did not make a problem statement, problem analysis and diagnosis, but simply followed orders. Maybe the sales engineers were right and custom modules were almost always needed (and maybe the potential of cost saving by standardization would anyway be limited). But the major problem was that the student did not involve the sales engineers in his problem-solving. The sales engineers did not recognize the problem, or at least that their own work might contribute to the problem of costs. They did not think along the same lines as the student. They were right in that the proposals derived from the tool were not directly usable, but with some manual adaptations that could have been corrected. They were not prepared to put effort into that, quite understandably, because it is more difficult to sell a semi-standard system than a fully customized one, a fact that would also have had a direct result on their pay, which included a commission on sales.

In terms of the theory of section 8.2 almost all sources of resistance to change were present:
– *lack of understanding*, although this was not the main source of resistance;
– certainly, as we have seen, *differences of opinion*;
– *lack of trust* in the student (especially in his insight in the commercial consequences of the use of his system);
– *low willingness of change*, both *inherent* (they did not see that they themselves might be a cause of the low profitability of the business unit; in their views it was the high costs of development and operations), as well as *induced low willingness to change*, as they were suddenly confronted with a new and possibly dangerous system, which had some support from management;
– finally, there was also much potential for *conflicts of interests*, as the system threatened to harm their material interests.

All that the student did in the face of this overwhelming (but, unfortunately for him, undetected) resistance to change, was a technical intervention: he gave a presentation of his system, fully expecting (like his supervisors) that the sales engineers would be happy that he had solved their problem.

To further understand why the student and his supervisors were surprised by the strong resistance on the part of the sales engineers, we need to provide further information. The resources of the business unit were geographically dispersed, with the development department near the university, and business unit management and marketing and sales one hour away by plane. If the problem had been named and framed as an inadequate marketing strategy, the student should have been placed within the marketing and sales department. However, it was named and framed as a technical problem (without much thought about implementation) so the student spent most of his time with the development department. During his project he had only a few meetings with the sales engineers, but these produced only feeble feedback because the sales engineers didn't believe it could be done. Eventually the very success of the student's work – in a technical sense – produced the fierce resistance discussed above.

Admittedly, it was a difficult assignment, both from a technical and an organizational change perspective, and more difficult than the IIS assignment. However, with careful preparation and good supervision it need not have failed. A sound problem analysis, shared with the sales engineers, might well have convinced them that a marketing strategy based on selling systems built from custom modules was untenable in the long run. That could have led to a discussion on standardization. It might be that the configurator was not such a good idea; maybe a marketing strategy based on customizing a limited range of standard key modules would have been better. But maybe it *was* a good idea, and, if the student had detected the resistance to his ideas towards the end of his project it might have been saved. Instead of presenting it as the new way of selling systems, he could have presented it as an exploration of the potential of standardization, triggering a discussion on the subject that could have led to valuable results for the company, with or without the configurator. As it was, in the discussions the only objective of the sales engineers was to scuttle the system, and in that fight the student was, of course, no match for them. Business problem-solving is not a technical-economic exercise, but a combination of technical-economic, political and cultural ones.

9 Evaluation, reflection and termination

9.1 Introduction

The final step of the regulative cycle is evaluation. Evaluation refers to the careful observation and appraisal of the process and the effects of a business problem-solving (BPS) project. An evaluation should tell whether a project is successfully completed, whether improvements need to be implemented, and what can be learnt for the future.

Unfortunately, many projects are terminated without an evaluation. For example, Von Zedtwitz (2002) found that eighty per cent of research and development projects are not evaluated. In projects that are executed by students there is some inevitability to this neglect. Due to their limited timeframe, these projects often do not finalize the implementation phase. If they do implement an object design, there is little time left for positive effects to be realized and measured. Even in projects that are not strictly limited in time, evaluation is often neglected. When a project is reaching its finalization, other projects loom ahead, which attract or require attention from the current project members. For the project members it may be more interesting to dive into a new project than to take a step back and contemplate the ongoing one. However, evaluation and reflection are highly valuable.

Evaluations can be performed with four objectives in mind. First, evaluations serve the current BPS project by determining the results achieved and the improvements to be made. This is evaluation in a strict sense. In a broader interpretation of evaluation, for which we shall use the term 'reflection', it serves three other objectives. Second, evaluation may also be oriented at learning for future problems. This use of evaluation and reflection is particularly stressed in the literature on organizational learning and knowledge management (see for example Busby 1999; Von Zedtwitz 2002). Third, evaluation and reflection can be oriented at advancing scientific knowledge about business processes.

Finally, evaluation and reflection are necessary for personal and professional development.

In line with their place in the regulative cycle, evaluation and reflection are typically carried out at the end of a project. However, given that evaluation and reflection include more than determining whether a problem has been solved, processes and intermediate products require evaluation and reflection as well. This enables the student to improve and change course on flight. Following the logic of the regulative cycle, we discuss evaluation and reflection as the final step, but it should be kept in mind that evaluation and reflection are desired at several moments during a project.

In the remainder of this chapter we discuss evaluation and reflection for each of the four different objectives. We end the chapter by addressing the termination of BPS projects and reporting about a project.

9.2 Project-oriented evaluation

When a solution or redesign is implemented in an organization, it is important to determine whether the original problem has indeed been solved. Have lead times been reduced to the desired level? Has internal knowledge-sharing been improved? Has customer satisfaction been increased? It is never certain whether or not a project has succeeded. The diagnosis may contain errors, oversights and uncertainties. The reasoning supporting an object design may be flawed or inaccurately incorporated in the object design. The object design may be implemented infelicitously. One or more of these potential sources of failure may hold for any particular project. We know quite a lot about organizations, but we can never know everything and there are few things we know beyond doubt. Thus, even if a BPS project is carried out according to the best possible standards and state-of-the-art theory, objectives still may not be achieved. Therefore, before closing a project, we need to know whether it has reached its goals.

Post-test only

Literature on evaluation makes a basic distinction between *pre-tests* and *post-tests* (for example Mohr 1995). A pre-test is a measurement of the targeted variable – that what is considered a problem and is intended to be changed – *before* a redesign has been implemented. A post-test is a measurement of the targeted variable *after* a redesign has been implemented.

The least informative way to evaluate implemented solutions is to execute a post-test only, to measure only after the fact. When only a post-test is done, there are no data to compare the results with, and it is impossible to determine whether there has been an improvement. Nevertheless, there are situations in which a post-test alone can be useful. When clear goals were formulated earlier in the project, the results of the post-test can be compared with these goals. Moreover, one can measure satisfaction with the implemented solution, and take this as a measure for the effectiveness of the solution.

Comparing pre-test with post-test

The most frequently used evaluation is the comparison of a pre-test with a post-test. Since this involves the comparison of the situation before and after a redesign has been implemented, this is also known as the 'before-after' design (Mohr 1995). This design is well suited to determine whether a performance improvement has taken place. The nature of the regulative cycle supports the use of a before-after evaluation design. One of the objectives of the diagnostic phase is to determine whether the supposed business problem really is a problem and, if so, how serious it is. This implies that a well-executed diagnosis yields the data that can later be interpreted as a pre-test, to be compared with the score on a post-test. This is an extra reason for determining the scope, frequency or seriousness of the business problem as objectively as possible in the diagnostic phase.

The before-after design can be extended by repeatedly measuring the score at the relevant performance criteria. Figure 9.1 displays such a series of scores at quality parameters of a logistic service provider, used to evaluate the impact of a project carried out in autumn 1996. A more continuous observation of performance parameters has advantages above the comparison of two obser-vations. A series of data makes it possible to distinguish between normal variation of a score and structural changes, and to inspect the impact of a redesign as a function of time. Figure 9.1 shows that, if only a single pre-test and a single post-test had been done, the results would have differed strongly depending on the exact moment of measurement. Now that a series of data is available, it is possible to conclude that there has been no strong effect from September 1996 onwards (if the data are interpreted benevolently, the positive trend continues, but it should be checked whether this is due to the same factors that caused the positive trend until September 1996).

The more objectives are stated in measurable terms, the more reliable and decisive an evaluation can be. However, objectives are often stated in more

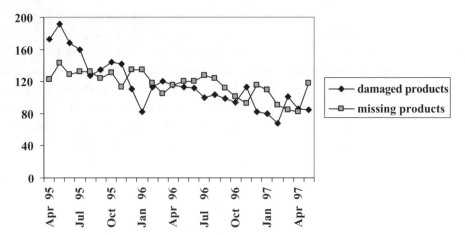

Figure 9.1   Number of damaged and missing products over a two-year period (data from a logistic service provider; Van Meurs 1997)

qualitative terms. To complicate things further, diagnoses are also frequently of a qualitative nature. Although there are good reasons for this (see Chapter 10) it makes it more difficult to compare the situation before and after implementation. The evaluation will probably be qualitative as well.

A limitation of a pre-test – post-test evaluation design is that it cannot determine the cause of an increase or decrease in performance. If the implementation of a redesign is not followed by enhanced performance, it could be because of shortcomings of the solution, or a bad implementation of the solution. There may even be other causes at work. For example, a marketing campaign may have a positive effect on sales figures, but there may be at the same time other factors such as an economic downturn, which diminish sales and therewith mask the positive effect of the campaign, potentially leading to a *false negative* conclusion. Likewise, if the comparison of a pre-test and a post-test shows a performance improvement, it is not necessarily the result of the implementation of a redesign. A famous example of such a *false positive* conclusion is provided by the Hawthorne investigations, studying, among other things, the effects of lighting on labour productivity. In this investigation, an increase in light intensity was accompanied by an increase in productivity, leading the researchers to believe that the increase in productivity was *caused* by the increase in light intensity. But when they decreased lighting again, productivity continued to increase, therewith falsifying the researchers' beliefs. Further investigations learned that it was not the light intensity that affected performance, but increased motivation of the workers due the fact that they felt valued and recognized by being the subject of the investigations (see also

Chapter 12 on internal validity). In the next paragraphs we will introduce comparative evaluation designs, which can overcome some of the threats to internal validity associated with the pre-test – post-test design.

Comparative post-test

In the previous section we explained that a post-test is more informative when compared with a pre-test. Another way to increase the value of a post-test score is to compare it with scores of other units, processes or organizations, in which the redesign has not been implemented. For example, the Dutch government defends its liberal policy on soft drugs by referring to the fact that there are fewer hard-drug addicts in the Netherlands than in countries with a more restrictive policy. This is an example of a *comparative post-test*: the post-test results of an entity that has undergone a particular intervention are compared with the results of the same test of an entity that has undergone no intervention or a different intervention. However, a threat to the validity of such an evaluation is that a difference in score may have existed before the implementation of a change program – in which case the difference in score would not reflect a positive effect of the implemented changes.

Comparative change design

This threat to validity can be reduced by using the *comparative change* design. A comparative change design evaluates the effect of the implementation of a redesign by comparing the difference between a pre-test and post-test with the difference between the scores of another organization, group or entity on the same tests. The comparative change design thus compares changes within a target group with changes that have occurred within a control group. Therefore, this design is also described as a quasi-experimental design. For example, one can compare changes in sales of a product for which a marketing campaign has been executed, with changes in sales of a comparable product for which no marketing campaign has been executed. Such a comparison prevents – for example – that an economic downturn masks the possible effect of a marketing campaign.

If the evaluation of results shows that the original problem has not yet been solved, there is a need to reassess the regulative cycle. If the original problem is still considered to be a problem, an improved redesign has to be implemented, based upon an improved diagnosis.

A first step towards an improved diagnosis is the execution of a formative evaluation. Scriven (cited in Mohr 1995) makes a distinction between formative evaluations and summative evaluations. Summative evaluations only focus on the measurement of the effect of a change program. In fact, the evaluation designs discussed above are all summative evaluations. Though summative evaluation is crucial, it does not tell us the whole story. In fact, it does not provide a story at all, just the ending. If a summative evaluation shows a negative outcome, we will particularly be interested in 'how' and 'why' questions. How did this low score come about? Why did people not behave according to our expectations? That is the kind of question that a formative evaluation intends to answer. A formative evaluation traces how the reasoning underlying a solution design and change plan has turned out in reality. It traces what sub-objectives have been accomplished and where the causal chain has broken down.

In the case of an unsuccessful project, a formative evaluation will show either that the redesign has not been implemented properly or that the reasoning underlying it was flawed. For instance, the implementation of a solution may have unintended consequences (Balogun and Johnson 2005). Take the following example. In order to reduce the layer of smog above the city of Athens in Greece, the city council decided that each car was allowed in the city only on every other day: cars with an even numberplate on even days, and cars with an odd numberplate on odd days. The basic reasoning supporting this measure was that car owners would choose public transport or car pooling on the days they were not allowed to drive, which would reduce exhaustive gasses by fifty per cent and thus reduce the layer of smog above the city. However, a formative evaluation proved this reasoning to be flawed: people who were used to driving by car, chose to buy another car with the alternative type of numberplate, so that they were always allowed to drive one of their two cars.

A formative evaluation that uncovers such unexpected flaws in the reasoning underlying a solution contributes to an enriched diagnosis. The diagnosis may be improved in other ways as well. It frequently happens that new ideas on the cause of problems come up during redesign and implementation. According to some authors, it is impossible to fully understand organizational processes without intervening in them. The social psychologist Kurt Lewin once stated 'If you want to truly understand something, try to change it'. Of course, the degree to which we are certain about the adequacy of the reasoning behind a solution differs. Especially under higher degrees of uncertainty, it is worthwhile to anticipate and exploit learning from implementation and evaluation. An easy way to do so is by using pilot implementations: trying out a solution in just one department, for instance.

Based upon an improved diagnosis, a new or improved redesign has to be developed and implemented. In some cases this may be a completely new solution. For example, if a doctor finds out that a medicine does not help a patient, he may decide to prescribe another medicine. In other cases fine-tuning of a solution is more appropriate. This is comparable with a doctor who changes the dose of a medicine. In either case the guidelines for implementation as presented in Chapter 8 apply. Especially after initial failure, support and involvement of organization members and managers is crucial.

9.3 Learning for the future

A second objective of evaluation and reflection is to learn for the future. Current organization theory stresses that technological knowledge and managerial capabilities are an important source of competitive advantage for a firm (Nonaka 1994). Given the importance of knowledge and capabilities for organizational performance, those firms that create and retain knowledge faster may be able to outperform others. Learning is the process in which knowledge and capabilities are developed. Therefore, organization theory has stressed the importance of organizational learning (Argyris and Schön 1978). Project evaluation and reflection on projects are important mechanisms to stimulate these learning processes (Busby 1999; Von Zedtwitz 2002).

For the purpose of learning, it does not matter whether a project has been successful or not. One can learn from successes and failures, from mindful actions as well as mistakes. A project that has not delivered the intended results may be painful for those involved, but that does not mean that it should be forgotten as soon as possible. Failures are a great source of learning. After the Spanish football club Barcelona lost the fourth game of football in a row – it was beaten six–three by Real Zaragosa – and was nine points behind with only a limited number of games to play, its coach Johan Cruijff told his players: 'Thanks to this defeat, we will win the league', And they did. By reflecting on failures, one can avoid others, or oneself, falling into the same trap another time. From a successful project one can learn how to do it next time. If lessons from a current project are captured, this prevents somebody else reinventing the wheel.

Both the outcome and the process of business problem-solving can be objects of learning. In our terms, it is possible to learn about object design, realization design and process design. The solution that was developed – the object design – may be relevant for other situations as well. It is also possible to learn from the implementation of this solution, about the change plan. What successful actions are to be retained and what actions should be avoided in the future? Finally, organizations benefit from building a capability in performing BPS projects. Given the abundance of problem-solving activities in organizations, people and organizations who are experienced and skilled in the execution of these projects, have a clear advantage. This implies that it is also important to learn about each of the process steps of the regulative cycle.

Unfortunately, people in organizations often think that experience is a sufficient condition for learning. This is not true. Learning from experience requires reflection. Without actively reflecting on experiences, only a limited part of potential lessons will be learnt (Simonin 1997). Yet, the degree to which reflection is necessary may differ. Some lessons are more easy to learn than others. For example, if a new type of solution is implemented, for everyone to see, and it is clear whether it is successful or not, it is easy to retain that insight for future use. Other actions are far less visible. Reflection is needed to articulate and conceptualize these actions and to externalize tacit knowledge.

Active reflection cannot change the fact that the effects of many actions are ambiguous. We often do not have enough information to conclude with certainty that a particular action had a particular effect. We are even less certain whether it would have the same effect in another situation and under different circumstances. Generalization is as problematic in post-project reflection as it is in scientific research (see also Chapter 12). Furthermore, the human mind is prone to a number of biases, including confirmation bias (the tendency to pay more attention to success than to failure). Thus, learning for the future is not an easy task.

Reflection may take place informally, but organizations may also institutionalize evaluation and reflection processes. Formal reflections are sometimes labelled 'post-project reviews'. Several methodologies for these post-project reviews are available (Von Zedtwitz 2002).

To reflect, people have to look at their own activities from a distance. However, this presents a paradoxical situation: you have to look at yourself from an outside perspective, but you can do this only from within your own 'head' and your own frame of reference. Reflection, therefore, is greatly enhanced by creating an external point of reference that can be used as a mirror, or as a stance from which to view oneself or one's project. Several ways exist to create an external point of reference. One may think of checklists for project

Box 9.1   Project implementation profile

An example of an instrument for the systematic monitoring of and reflection on projects is provided by Slevin and Pinto (1986). They propose that project managers evaluate projects monthly on ten dimensions:
- clarity of project mission and goals;
- top management support;
- availability of a project schedule/plan;
- consultation with the client and other impacted parties;
- recruitment, selection and training of personnel;
- availability of required technology;
- client acceptance;
- monitoring and feedback;
- communication between all key actors;
- ability to handle unexpected crises and deviations.

management (see box 9.1), methodological criteria (see Chapter 12) or a theoretical perspective like team roles. Viewing project members, activities and outcomes from external points of reference will not provide immediate answers, but will help to raise questions. Questions are a necessary input for reflection, since they steer attention, urge to externalize tacit habits and insights, and provide a basis for discussion.

Another way to bring in an external point of reference is to involve others in reflection. The role of others in reflection is not to transfer their knowledge, but to assist in the reflective process by 'thinking along' (Berends *et al* 2004). Others may help by coming up with new suggestions or detecting imperfections. A particularly appropriate way of supporting reflection is asking questions. Others frequently come up with questions one has not thought about. Furthermore, if you talk to others, you need to structure your own thoughts and you are forced to formulate arguments for your own position.

Having others contribute to reflection by thinking along can be organized in different ways. It is always possible to take initiative yourself for informal interactions. Yet, several institutionalized opportunities for reflection with others exist. Examples are:
- sessions with the platform group (if present);
- presentation and discussion of projects, problems and results in colloquia and seminars;
- periodical meetings with a coach, mentor or supervisor;
- participation in communities-of-practice (Wenger 1998) and peer consultation groups (De Haan 2004);

The results of learning through evaluation and reflection need to be retained in some way in order to be used in the future. Furthermore, what has been learned at the individual level or at the group level should be made more broadly available – if relevant – in order to turn individual learning into organizational learning (Huber 1991). The recent field of knowledge management has particularly investigated how to capture, share and re-use knowledge (Davenport and Prusak 1998; Newell *et al* 2002). Some organizations, including consultancy firms and research and development departments, have a tradition of writing reports on finished projects. Today, many larger organizations have an intranet, containing descriptions and evaluations of BPS projects. The recent knowledge management literature has also stressed the importance of informal contacts and direct cooperation as valuable ways to share knowledge. Especially in the case of tacit knowledge and skills that are hard to put in words, informal interactions are more suited for knowledge-sharing than explicit reports (Nonaka 1994).

9.4 Scientific reflection

An organization will be first and foremost interested in what it can learn from a project for its own future. Students who carry out a BPS project are also expected, to a greater or lesser degree, to reflect on a project from a scientific perspective. Basically, this boils down to a comparison of the project with current literature on similar problems, and determining what this particular case can add to the literature. That contribution can be written up for a scientific paper or an article for a professional journal.

Reflection on a single case can contribute in four ways to the existing literature: as innovation, elaboration, verification and falsification. We will discuss these subsequently.

Innovation

Firstly, something new may be discovered or developed within the project. This is a potentially innovative contribution to the scholarly literature. Given that projects that follow the regulative cycle are oriented towards problem-solving, it is likely that an innovative contribution, if any, lies in a new type of solution. Nevertheless, it is also possible to discover a new phenomenon in the problem analysis step. Furthermore, it is possible to come up with a new or adapted method of data collection or a new way of describing a business process. Of course, the fact that something has been established as valid, adequate or useful in one single case does not guarantee that it holds as well for other cases. It is easy to see the threats of generalizing from one case to others. Whether the solution, phenomenon or method applies to other cases as well is an open question or a hypothetical claim. When it is presented in the scientific literature, others are able to check the hypothesis and to elaborate upon it.

Elaboration

Secondly BPS projects often do not yield radically new solutions, but elaborations of existing designs and theories. The application of theory in BPS projects is seldom straightforward. Theoretical schemes need to be tailored to the specific characteristics of the situation or combined with each other. Though this often proves to be troublesome when diagnosing or redesigning, it creates the opportunity to contribute to the literature afterwards. It will be interesting for organizations facing comparable problems to learn about the way a particular theory was made applicable, or how a solution concept was contextualized to suit a specific situation. Therefore, this type of contribution will be relevant for professional journals and more accessible scientific journals. Top-level scientific journals are likely to consider the degree of novelty too limited.

Verification

A third type of contribution is the confirmation or verification of existing claims. If a particular theory or solution has not yet been applied in a real-life situation, or when such an application has not yet been described in the literature, there is scientific merit in reporting its successful application. This strengthens the evidence in favour of this theory. If the approach has been tested many times before, it is less likely that others are interested in learning that it has worked. A stronger contribution can be made by figuring out whether the project has unique characteristics. Readers of professional journals may be interested, since they are always keen on practical experiences with more abstract concepts and, in contrast to readers of scientific journals, care less whether comparable experiences have been described before.

Falsification

A fourth way to contribute to the literature is to present findings that contradict claims in the existing literature. For example, a student may find that a solution concept that was presented in the literature proved to be ineffective when applied in practice. The refutation of existing claims has been called 'falsification' by the philosopher of science Popper (1963). According to Popper, falsification plays a central role in the growth of our knowledge. If we learn that a theory or design is not adequate, we are encouraged to search for better theories and designs. However, falsification beyond doubt, as Popper liked to have it, is hard to realize. Proponents of the original claim may defend it by pointing at the specific characteristics of the current project: they may argue that the fact that their solution did not work is due to the unsuitability of this specific case, or that the solution has not been implemented properly.

Scientific reflection on BPS projects is often considered a bonus, if done at all. These projects are driven by a business problem and not by a scientific problem. It is also possible to start a particular BPS project with a scientific contribution in mind. This is the case when management science is conducted as a design science (Van Aken 2004). Particular instances of problem-solving according to the regulative cycle will be subordinated to a reflective cycle (see Chapter 4), aimed at the production of more general guidelines or 'technological rules'. Consultancy firms and university staff in particular are able to compare different BPS projects executed by consultants or students, and use this comparison for the development of more general insight.

9.5 Personal and professional development

Evaluation and reflection do not only serve the client organization or management science. High-performing professionals are also aware that they need to learn continuously. Professionals can learn from each of the projects in which they are involved. They can learn which solutions to use or not. For that purpose, they can use the project evaluation and the scientific reflection, if any. In that way they can develop their knowledge and professional skills or keep them state-of-the-art. Personal and professional development will be further enhanced when experiences themselves are steered as well. A complementary activity of reflection is *deliberate practice* (Van der Wiel *et al* 2004). Deliberate practice refers to the conscious actions taken to improve a particular practice, be it the mastery of a musical instrument or the execution of business improvement projects. Deliberate practice steers experiences in such a way that more can be learned from them.

Reflection can teach professionals more about themselves. Reflection may be oriented at an underlying level of beliefs, values and unconscious habits.

It can help you to identify your strengths and weaknesses, which type of work you enjoy and which you do not, and how you best interact with other people. Such reflections are not tied to a particular phase in a project. You can be confronted with consequences of your actions, habits and personality at any moment. Sometimes you will have to align your actions with your beliefs. Sometimes you will have to question your beliefs. That is not the easiest thing to do. Over the last years more and more courses are offered for managers, consultants and other professionals to learn to reflect critically on their functioning. Furthermore, at several places peer consultation groups with the same goal have been created. Examples of this practice are described in Driehuis (1997) and De Haan (2004).

Up to this point we have predominantly taken an instrumental perspective on evaluation and reflection: learning about the effectiveness of our actions towards the resolution of problems. However, in reflection we may also question the social and political status quo in which a project has been executed. Who has benefitted from the project? Has it been at the expense of others? How independently have I functioned from management? Should that be more or less?

9.6 Project termination and reporting

Professional project management includes attention to the termination of a project. The termination does not refer to the last handshake, but to the whole process of winding up the project. Projects executed by students usually have a fixed duration, but that does not imply that the termination of a project is an automatic achievement. Terminating a project mindfully means that activities are planned in such a way that the time of departure is logical from the perspective of the deliverables of the project. The client organization should be able to proceed on its own with the deliverables produced in the BPS project.

An important element of the termination of a project is reporting. The final report on the project is intended to provide justification for proposed solutions and the documentation of the project. The justification is needed for the final decision-making on the solution (and where necessary to convince possible stakeholders outside the final decision-making process). The documentation is needed for the implementation and use of the solution. The final report should contain no news for the principal and other organization members who were strongly involved in the project. The moment of termination is not the moment to propose solutions and change plans. Analyses and proposals should already have been communicated through intermediate reports, presentations and other channels. A final report can only play a minor role in the change management process. If no support has been developed before the distribution of the report, the report is likely to be a paper tiger: it may seem to contain powerful ideas, but will end in a drawer.

As the final report should provide the justification for proposals, it should essentially follow the logic of the regulative cycle, as this cycle is oriented at the development of justified designs. Thus, the report may contain sections on problem definition, methodology, diagnosis, redesign, implementation and evaluation. In order to make the project comprehensible for outsiders and to sketch the strategic context, a company introduction is required. The report may contain a theoretical section, but theory may also be interwoven in the other sections, as theory does not have an independent role in a BPS project.

Because a final report is essentially oriented at the justification and documentation of proposed solutions and change plans, the report should be logical instead of chronological. That is, the report should not necessarily follow the sequence in which activities were undertaken. Employing concepts from the German philosopher Reichenbach (1938), the report is located within the *context of justification*, not the *context of discovery*. For justification purposes, processes of discovery and creation have to be rationally reconstructed. For example, analysis and design activities that were tried but eventually not used should not be included (although reference may be made to the fact that they were used yet abandoned). Analyses and design activities that were undertaken later in time may be presented earlier in the report, if that makes the reasoning more logical.

Finally, the termination of a project presents an opportunity for the consolidation of the relationship with the client organization. If organizations are satisfied with the work of students – and often they are – it may be valuable to explore opportunities for future projects, either for oneself or for future students. Educational institutions benefit from long-term relationships with organizations, as this enables easy access to the field and enables projects to build upon earlier projects. Whether or not the relationship is continued, students and supervisors should thank client organizations for offering the opportunity to carry out a BPS project, as the feasibility of BPS projects depends on their willingness to offer students access to real-life business problems.

Part III

On methods

In this part we discuss various methods to be used in business problem-solving (BPS) projects and the quality criteria with respect to the knowledge obtained though the application of these methods.

10 Qualitative research methods

10.1 Qualitative versus quantitative

The literature on methodology distinguishes between *qualitative* and *quantitative* research methods. The phrase 'qualitative' does not refer to the quality of methods. Qualitative methods are those that are oriented at the discovery of qualities of things, that is, the properties of objects, phenomena, situations, people, meanings and events. In contrast, quantitative methods are oriented at the number or amount of these qualities. This chapter will discuss a number of qualitative research methods that can be used in business problem-solving (BPS) projects. For quantitative research methods we refer the reader to text books on social science methodology such as Cooper and Schindler (2003) and Ader and Mellenbergh (1999).

Imagine a marketing manager who would like to know the opinions of potential customers about a television commercial. He could ask some respondents to talk freely about their feelings with regard to the commercial, their associations, what they like about it and what not, and so on. Such a study would be qualitative in nature, since it aims to uncover the characteristics of people, in this case their attitude towards the commercial. The same marketing manager could also use a standardized questionnaire and ask respondents to express the degree to which they understand and like the commercial on a five-point scale. Such a study would be quantitative in nature since it measures the amount of a particular property.

Qualitative research methods are particularly important if one intends to study people, groups, organizations and societies. For example, if you want to learn how people interpret their own situation, what their goals in life and work are, and what strategies they employ to reach those goals. Because there can be large and multifaceted differences between people, it is often not effective to employ a standardized measuring instrument.

Qualitative research methods are not only relevant within the social sciences. The natural and technical sciences use qualitative methods as well. Hendrik Casimir, a respected physicist and long-time director of Philips Laboratories, stated: 'For although it is certainly true that quantitative measurements are of great importance, it is a grave error to suppose that the whole of experimental physics can be brought under this heading. We can start measuring only when we know what to measure: qualitative observation has to precede quantitative measurement, and by making experimental arrangements for quantitative measurements we may even eliminate the possibility of new phenomena appearing.' (Casimir 1983: 161.)

Some authors define qualitative methods in a more specific manner. For example, it is claimed that a study is qualitative when the research data consist of texts of which the textual nature is retained in analysis. Examples of textual data are interview transcripts, notes of observations and existing documents. We will discuss these types of data in the next section.

Finally, some methodologists associate qualitative methods solely with specific paradigmatic assumptions. According to them, qualitative research is characterized by an interpretative approach: 'looking through the eyes of somebody else'. They consider a study qualitative when it aims at understanding another person, group or culture. We will not use the phrase 'qualitative methods' in this limited way. But we agree with the assumption that if you want to understand the perspective of somebody else, you will first need to employ qualitative research methods.

In the remainder of this chapter we will first discuss the choice for a unit of analysis (section 10.2) and strategies to select cases (section 10.3). In section 10.4 we will discuss data collection methods. Interviews are by far the most popular qualitative data collection technique. They are often used without much reflection. However, we will describe other qualitative data collection techniques and argue that those may be more useful in particular situations. In section 10.5 we will turn to qualitative methods for the analysis of data. The chapter ends with some reflections on the choice for particular methods.

10.2 Unit of analysis

Before engaging on the task of collecting data, one has to determine the *unit of analysis*. Confronted with organizational reality, some students are overwhelmed by the mass of potential data, or do not see potential data at all. In order to be able to select data and guide analysis, the unit of analysis has to be chosen. The unit of analysis is the type of object that is the focus of interest. Several objects can be the unit of analysis in a BPS project. We will discuss the most important options below. Which one is suited for a BPS project depends on the particular characteristics of the business problem involved. The unit of analysis that is chosen should be strongly related to the problem. The problem should exhibit itself, or become realized, through those objects.

Orders and projects

The most natural unit of analysis in BPS projects is usually the item that is produced or realized within a business process: orders, products or projects. Business problems are directly connected with such 'objects'. Many operations management problems are fruitfully approached via the study of production, sales or shipping orders. Innovation management problems can be studied well through specific innovation projects. The same holds for project-based organizations like building contractors. If an order or a project is chosen as the unit of analysis, the student should determine the performance of each case and find causes of deficiencies. This can be done through cross-case analysis, for example by comparing successes with failures.

Events, incidents, decisions and interactions

Other potential units of analysis have an event-like character. One may for example study decisions and decision processes or interactions between individuals or groups. Incidents are a similar unit of analysis, often useful in BPS projects. A specific method that centres on incidents is the *critical incident technique*.

The *critical incident technique* (CIT) is developed to obtain more insight in the execution of tasks by employees. For example, the CIT can be used to discover what factors influence the successful completion of tasks, what behaviour is effective under particular circumstances, and what skills employees need to execute the task. In order to do so, employees who execute that task are requested to report critical incidents. Critical incidents are events in which something went wrong, went nearly wrong or went particularly well. Those critical incidents are often much more informative than 'business-as-usual'. The data on incidents can be gathered through interviews, but also through focus groups, questionnaires and diaries. Flanagan (1954) contains the original presentation of the CIT. Chell (1998) writes about the diversity of ways in which the CIT has been applied in management research.

Wim van Vuuren (1993) applied the CIT in his graduation project. His project was oriented at discovering causes of near misses (situations that could have turned into an accident), with the ultimate aim of preventing real accidents. He asked employees of the steel company Hoogovens (now Corus) to narrate about recently occurred near misses. Together with the interviewees he constructed a cause-and-effect tree for each incident. The root causes of the incidents were analyzed with an existing classification scheme. In this way, he could trace the origin of near misses and determine the relative importance of different types of causes. This information could be used to take better safety precautions. By choosing the incident as the unit of analysis, data collection and analysis were directly related to the safety problem.

Organizational units

There are also business problems for which it is more natural to take an organizational unit (individuals, teams, departments and so on) as the unit of analysis. For example, if the business problem concerns motivation or satisfaction, individual employees are an appropriate unit of analysis. If a qualitative research approach is chosen, individual employees can be selected as cases to be studied and compared. Other types of organizational units that may be chosen as unit of analysis are teams, departments or business units. One may also think of clients and stakeholders as units of analysis (Burgoyne 1994). The following example gives yet another type of organizational unit that can be the focus of interest.

A recent project within Rolls-Royce (Meeuwesen 2005) focused on the limited learning output of communities of practice (CoPs). CoPs are informal groups of employees who work in different departments and geographical locations but within the same specialty. In this project it was natural to take the CoP as the unit of analysis, and five CoPs, which differed with regard to their performance, were compared.

Business process or organizational system

The last option is to take the whole subject of research as the unit of analysis. If the subject of research is a particular business process, that whole process can be considered as the unit of analysis. In that case there is no need to compare different cases as there are no different cases of the unit of analysis.

Within one project, different units of analysis may be combined – as long as those different units of analysis are dealt with separately. For example, one may study a number of projects as well as the department in which those projects are executed. Characteristics of that department are likely to influence each of the projects in the same way and cross-case analysis may not reveal that influence or may not yield a systematic analysis of those department-level characteristics.

10.3 Case selection

If an appropriate unit of analysis has been chosen and one intends to study multiple cases (multiple projects, orders, decisions, and so on), specific cases of that type of object have to be selected for further investigation. The diagnosis of a BPS project often includes a cross-case analysis. The same may hold for an evaluation. For example, the project at Rolls-Royce, referred to above, included a comparison of five CoPs. In a similar vein, orders, incidents and organizational units may be compared.

The selection of cases may be based upon pragmatic grounds. The number of cases that are available may be limited, or there may be only a few cases for which data can be obtained easily. If more cases are available, selection should occur on theoretical grounds.

Case selection on theoretical grounds can be driven by considerations about *independent variables* or about *dependent variables*. In BPS analysis dependent variables are the performance characteristics of cases, and independent variables are those characteristics that may affect that performance. A selection based on one or more independent variables means that case selection is based upon potential causes (Swanborn 1996). For example, if a company experiences a problem with regard to products that are out of stock, and expects a difference between fast-moving and slow-moving products, it may select both cases of fast movers and slow movers. This is an example of creating heterogeneity on the independent variable. If an initial cause-and-effect tree has been constructed in the orientation phase, it may help to determine on what dimensions cases should differ. However, it is not a necessity to select cases that differ on the independent variables. If one does not expect different outcomes for different cases, one does not need to strive for variety on the independent variable. Cases may be selected on other grounds and one may search for similarities that explain performance deficiencies.

Case selection can also be driven by considerations about dependent variables. As BPS projects are concerned with explaining insufficient performance, one may select both unsuccessful cases and successful cases (for example projects that exceeded budget and projects that stayed within budget) and investigate differences. The selection of cases may also be limited to unsuccessful cases in order to search for commonalities between those cases. However, there are some potential pitfalls associated with selecting on the success of cases. First, the success of cases is sometimes hard to establish in advance, without a detailed examination. Second, the identification of a case as a success or a failure is likely to influence perceptions about other characteristics of the case.

Not all cases have to be selected in advance. Qualitative methodologists frequently argue that the selection of new cases should be based on results of cases that have already been executed (Yin 1994; Glaser and Strauss 1967). The first cases that a researcher executes make it clear what dimensions of the cases are relevant. New cases can be selected in order to replicate the findings of earlier cases or to test hypotheses that result from earlier cases.

10.4 Qualitative data collection methods

This section gives an overview of different methods that can be used for the collection of qualitative data. Those data are the 'raw material' for research. Some methodologists prefer to speak of 'capta' instead of 'data'. Data refers to what is given. However, data are often not given, but need to be created or captured. That is for example the case in interviews. In this section we will discuss data collection techniques only briefly. For each of these techniques we will also refer to sources in which they are described more extensively. As you will notice, many of the articles we refer to are collected in *Qualitative Methods in Organizational Research: A Practical Guide* (Cassell and Symon 1994) and *Qualitative Methods and Analysis in Organizational Research: A Practical Guide* (Symon and Cassell 1998).

The interview

In practically all BPS projects, interviewing is one of the main methods of data gathering. There is much literature on this subject (see for example King 1994; Kvale 1996). Within the scope of this handbook we will confine ourselves to a few practicalities.

First of all, preparation is important. In many cases one needs a series of interviews. First one needs to formulate one or more overall research questions, then draw up a list of possible informants, both inside and outside the client organization, and define an outline of what one wants to know from each informant. After that one makes a specific interview guide for each interview. In most cases a semi-structured approach is used, using a list of specific questions but leaving sufficient room for additional information. In the preparation one should also analyze the perspective of the informant on the problem at hand, in order to be sensitive for possible personal and positional bias in the answers.

The interviews must be introduced to the informant by the principal of the BPS project, or someone near it. The project may already have been introduced to the informant, in which case a specific introduction of the interview itself may not be needed and the problem-solver can make an appointment for the interview in person.

In conducting the interview, interviewers have a dual role. They have a content-oriented role, aimed at getting clear and unbiased answers to the research questions, and a management role, aimed at managing the interview, that is aimed at managing the time spent on the various issues and at maintaining an open and, as far as possible, pleasant atmosphere, among other things by showing that the informant is giving an important contribution to the solution of the business problem in question.

At the start of the interview the problem-solver will introduce the BPS project and its background, what the objectives of the interview are, and why the interview is important to the BPS project. Also the issue of confidentiality must be mentioned (usually the results of the interviews will be presented to others anonymously) and how the results of the interview will be fed back to the interviewee to check them.

Leave room towards the end of the interview for additional information. Conclude the interview with some general remarks, bringing the specific results from the interview into the perspective of the overall BPS project. Thank the interviewee, and make an agreement on how and when to provide feedback to them, both of the results of the interview (among other things to check them) and of the results of the BPS project.

Focus groups

Usually we think of interviews as being held with one respondent. Nevertheless, in some situations it may be more effective to interview more people at the same time. Such an interview of a group of people is often called a 'focus group'. Focus groups are frequently used in market research. An advantage of focus groups is that they provide more insight in differences and similarities among the opinions of group members. It is more likely that one gets to know what options are truly intersubjectively shared. Furthermore, the remarks of others stimulate interviewees to clarify themselves and give further explanation. A disadvantage of focus groups is that people can be inhibited and less open than in a personal interview. Focus groups can be used at several points in BPS projects. They can be valuable within a diagnosis, but also in redesign and evaluation. More explanation on the use of focus groups can be found in Steyaert and Bouwen (1994) and Morgan (1991).

Documentation

In many BPS projects it is helpful to use existing documents as a source of information. Think for example of annual reports, minutes of meetings, mission statements, policy documents, incident reports, procedures, memos, correspondence and all kinds of databases. An important advantage of documentation is that it may provide information that organization members have partly or completely forgotten. Furthermore, corporate documentation is often a more reliable source of information than the opinion of an organization member. An important disadvantage of documentation is that it does not allow you to ask any additional question. You have to make do with what you have found. For more information on documentation as a source of data in an interpretative study, Forster (1994) is a good starting point.

(Participative) observation

Anthropologists studying another culture often do so by spending a lot of time within the community they are focusing on. By participating in daily activities, one is enabled to experience life from an insider's perspective. Participant observation is also used in management studies. For example, in order to uncover what it is like to do particular work. In some cases, the researcher does not even tell others that he is studying them. A popular example of this type of research is the book *Ich (Ali)* written by Günther Wallraff, about the ruthless exploitation of migrant workers in Germany.

BPS projects are often characterized by some degree of participative observation. The student becomes to some extent a member of the organization, joins meetings and lunch breaks and may even participate in operational activities. Participative observation enables the student to experience organizational processes from within.

To reap the full value of observations, they need to be captured in some way. This can be done by taking notes of observations, but also by recording meetings, events or actions on audiotape or videotape. Observation can also be used in quantitative research, for example by counting how often particular events take place. The time-and-motion studies developed in the era of scientific management are a classic example. More information about participative observation can be found in Spradley (1980), Van Maanen (1988), Waddington (1994) and Nason and Golding (1998).

Verbal protocols

If it is necessary to know exactly how people act in a particular situation and why they act as they do, verbal protocols may be considered as a data collection technique. Verbal protocols are records of thinking aloud sessions. A lot of research into problem-solving and human-computer interaction has used verbal protocols. For example, someone learning to use a new piece of software may be asked to verbalize any thought that crosses his mind while struggling with the software. Ericsson and Simon (1984) have written a book that is the classical source on verbal protocols. Johnson and Briggs (1994) have written about the use of verbal protocols in organizational research.

Diaries

Another qualitative method for data gathering is to have respondents keep a diary on a particular topic. You may ask organization members to record specific incidents that you are interested in or let them track their activities during a day. An advantage of keeping a diary above interviews is that people often forget important details or even misrepresent them during interviews. Furthermore, information gathered through diaries lends itself rather easily for use in quantitative analysis. Different ways of using diaries are described in Symon (1998).

10.5 Qualitative methods of analysis

Collecting data is not an end in itself. Within a BPS project data are collected to arrive at a description or an explanation of a business problem. At the beginning of a project, interviews will be held to gain insight into the problem mess. Later, a student needs a description of the business processes that are involved in the problem and an explanation of the occurrence of the problem. That is, the student aims at uncovering the causes of the problem. In order to arrive at these descriptions and explanations, the data that were gathered have to be analyzed.

The collection of qualitative data often yields a huge pile of raw material. Sometimes it is suggested that the analysis of those qualitative data is an intractable, subjective process, thriving upon the intuition of the researcher. Indeed, too many qualitative studies do not explain how raw data were turned into findings and conclusions. In this section we will explain that the analysis of qualitative data does not need to be intractable, but can be done in systematic ways. We discern two strategies to analyze qualitative data: the grounded theory approach and the template approach. Basically, the grounded theory approach is data-driven and the template approach is more theory-driven. These strategies will be discussed subsequently in the remainder of this chapter.

Grounded theory approach

The grounded theory approach is a structured approach for the exploration of unfamiliar territory. It is a method to develop theory out of raw qualitative data in a systematic way. 'Theory' refers to a coherent set of concepts and relationships between those concepts that represents a particular aspect of reality (instead of 'theory' it is often also appropriate to speak of a 'model'). Thus, the grounded theory approach aims at the development of concepts and relationships between concepts.

In the diagnostic phase of the regulative cycle the student aims at the development of what can be called a mini-theory or a local theory. One of the characteristics of working in accordance with the regulative cycle is that it is oriented at a unique situation. The student is oriented at a particular problem in a particular organization and not at a class of problems in a class of organizations. Therefore the student develops a model or a theory of that particular case and not a general theory. A local theory, so to say. This local theory can be both descriptive and explanatory. The concepts within such a local theory will include relevant problems, causes and possible strategic consequences.

The grounded theory approach employs three central procedures: *open coding, theoretical coding* and *selective coding*. These procedures will be discussed in the following sections.

Open coding

Coding is measuring at a nominal level. This means that a concept is attached to a phenomenon. In ordinary language, coding can be described as labelling or categorizing something. A characteristic of open coding is that it does not use an existing coding scheme. Codes are developed while coding. In this way, the student does not straitjacket data. The main guide for attaching a code to a piece of data are the data themselves. While reflecting on a piece of data – be it an interview transcript, a document or observation notes – you should ask yourself: what is this about? The answer to that question should be framed in one or more codes. You can choose these codes yourself. The only criterion for attaching a code is that it fits the data.

The grounded theory approach offers two strategies to aid open coding: asking questions and comparing data. Because the grounded theory approach is normally used for exploratory purposes, it is impossible to ask very specific questions. Asking only specific questions would straitjacket the discovery process. What can be done however, is to ask more general questions: what is this situation about?, What problem is this person addressing?, What property is expressed in these data?

The second strategy to aid open coding is the making of comparisons. Because making comparisons is important in the grounded theory approach, it is also called the 'method of constant comparison'. During open coding, pieces of data – concerning different people, processes or situations – are compared. Characteristics of a person, process or situation become clearer if it is compared with others. Comparing them shows differences and similarities and stimulates the researcher to put these into words.

Data have to be sliced into pieces for open coding. A strategic question with regard to open coding is the size of the fragments to be coded. It is possible to code sentences, larger fragments or complete documents. The grounded theory approach considers all of these options legitimate. Of course, one has to take care that the amount of codes that are generated is limited to a manageable number (yet, in theoretical studies, it is not exceptional to develop up to 100 codes). If one has developed many codes, similar codes can be grouped into categories. Categories are also concepts, but on a more abstract level.

Theoretical coding

The second analytical procedure of the grounded theory approach is theoretical coding. A theory consists of concepts and relationships between those concepts. Concepts are developed in open coding. Theoretical coding is oriented toward the discovery of relationships between concepts. Theoretical coding consists of putting relationships into words. These relationships can take many forms. A causal relationship is only one of them. One concept may also be a property of another, be a prerequisite for another, be followed in time by another, or be part of the context of another. Glaser (1978) distinguishes eighteen families of types or relations.

Within the local theory that is developed in the diagnostic phase different types of relationships can be used. An Ishikawa diagram can be interpreted as a local theory consisting of cause-effect relations. Another type of relation is sequential. Two concepts can refer to activities that follow each other within a business process. Such sequential relations are central to flow charts of business processes, which can be interpreted as local theories as well.

Theoretical coding should be grounded in data too. Students should search the data to find indications for the existence of relationships. As Glaser (1978; 1992) argues, these will be found. Human interaction is not chaotic, but patterned. Interviewees themselves may indicate relationships. Also, the analyst may see a certain relation between two codes. In both cases the theoretical relationship will be of a hypothetical nature. In theoretical coding one is always working inductively, generalizing from individual incidents to more general patterns.

Logically, theoretical coding follows open coding. Before one is able to draw relationships, one needs to have concepts. But in the practice of coding these processes will be done in parallel and iteratively.

Selective coding

The third procedure advocated by the grounded theory approach is selective coding. Selective coding is meant to elaborate concepts and relationships found during open coding and theoretical coding. Selective coding does not aim at the development of new concepts but at the crystallization of results. Selective coding presupposes that the student scans the data for not-yet-analyzed instances of a particular phenomenon or relationship. The student may also go back to the field to selectively gather new data. The grounded theory approach uses preferably an integration of data collection and data analysis. Only during coding does it become clear precisely what the research will be about. Having preliminary concepts and hypotheses enables the researcher to ask more specific questions. The process of selective coding, and grounded theory analyses in general, can be stopped when concepts and relations are *saturated*, that is when additional collection and analysis of data no longer lead to new insights. *Saturation* signals that the local theory is finished.

This section has explained the central characteristics of the grounded theory approach. If you decide to start working in accordance with this method, it is advisable to study the procedures of the grounded theory approach in more detail. A useful introduction is offered by Strauss and Corbin (1998).

Template approach

The grounded theory approach starts with an open perspective and does not presuppose much theoretical pre-understanding. In contrast, the template approach utilizes existing concepts and theories. The template approach assumes that students know in advance in which phenomena they want to create new insight. The conceptualization of these phenomena is the template for analyzing data. Miles and Huberman (1994) present a large collection of template-based techniques to structure and analyze data.

The template approach also employs a process of coding, but in contrast to the grounded theory approach, the template approach uses existing codes. If one has coded with these existing codes, all parts of interviews that are relevant for a particular code can be placed in a cell of a matrix. If different aspects are analyzed at the same time, different people or groups may be placed in the rows and different aspects in the columns. The cells of such a matrix contain information about a particular person or group with regard to a particular phenomenon. In this way one is forced to display data in a systematic way. Such a systematic display of data enables a more structured and valid analysis.

10.6 Selecting a method

We started this chapter by making a distinction between qualitative and quantitative methods. We then presented methods for data collection and data analysis. This final section addresses the selection of a method out of the array of possibilities. None of these methods is suited for all circumstances. Each method is suited for one group of settings, but not for another group of settings.

A rule of thumb for the choice between a qualitative and quantitative approach is to count whatever is reasonably countable. Whether it is possible to count depends upon three factors: (a) the nature of the phenomenon, (b) the knowledge one already has about that phenomenon, and (c) practical circumstances. Some objects are easy to count. Money is a familiar example of such an object. Other phenomena, like attitudes, are much less easy to count. Furthermore, one needs a certain level of pre-understanding about a phenomenon in order to be able to count it. Qualitative understanding precedes quantitative analysis. Even to count money, one needs to know what counts as money. If you know which three aspects of a car are considered to be most important by potential buyers, you can ask them to score a particular car on these aspects. Without pre-understanding, the choice for three scores would very likely be prejudiced. Finally, practical considerations play a role as counting may be possible in principle but not in practice.

The choice between approaches to the analysis of qualitative data should be guided by comparable considerations. As a rule of thumb, the most structured approach that is feasible should be chosen. In general, the more structured a study is, the more controllable and reliable it is. However, whether a structured approach is feasible depends upon the nature of the phenomena that one is interested in and the level of pre-understanding. By choosing concepts and procedures in advance, one harms validity by overlooking important aspects or straitjacketing data.

It is important to realize that methods do not exclude each other, but may be used in combination, either at the same time or sequentially. By triangulating qualitative and quantitative data, reliability can be increased (see Chapter 12). Qualitative analysis can also be used as a stepping stone for quantitative analysis.

In this chapter we have provided an overview of qualitative methods and techniques for collecting and analyzing data. If you want to use one of these methods, this introduction will be insufficient. We strongly recommend searching for more specific literature on the methods of choice. For that reason we have included references to other sources for each of the methods. If you compare two books or articles on any method, you will notice that each author gives a slightly different interpretation of the basic ideas. This illustrates that a method is not a code of law that should be followed by the letter, but should be tailored to each specific situation.

11 Searching and using scholarly literature

11.1 Introduction

No two business problem-solving (BPS) projects are identical. Yet, no business problem is completely different from all other business problems. Given the long history of management research, it is likely that problems comparable to a specific business problem have been studied already. As we have explained, BPS projects benefit from the use of this existing scholarly literature. Though the literature will not provide all of the answers, it can inform each of the steps of a BPS project. In this chapter we will be concerned with the search and use of existing scientific knowledge.

There is a widely shared concern that existing knowledge within the field of management science (and within other fields) is insufficiently used by practitioners (Van Aken 2004). One reason for this lies in the organization of knowledge. Management science literature is fragmented and contested (Whitley 1984; Tranfield *et al* 2003). It is fragmented, since relevant ideas and research findings are often scattered across different journals and fields of study, presented in different conceptual guises, and show little accumulation. Management literature is contested since studies that address comparable questions often yield contradictory results. Conflicting opinions co-exist – sometimes in mutual ignorance – and disputes often remain unsolved.

The fragmented and contested nature of knowledge on management interacts in a vicious cycle with the use of existing knowledge. Literature reviews in the field of management science are often of poor quality: they are ad hoc, unsystematic, biased by personal preferences, and do not contribute to the accumulation of knowledge (Tranfield *et al* 2003). Literature reviews are seldom undertaken with the same methodological rigor as empirical research. This sloppy practice of reviewing contributes to the fragmented and contested nature of management knowledge, which in turn complicates the use of that knowledge.

Yet, the last years have witnessed a growing concern about the development of methods for the systematic review and utilization of existing research (for example Cooper and Hedges 1993; Pawson 2002a; Tranfield *et al* 2003). The aim of this chapter is to provide an introduction to these methods and thereby aid the student, whose first dive in the literature is often an overwhelming experience. The *systematic review* of the literature enables a BPS project to benefit optimally from existing knowledge on a subject. In addition, systematic reviews may enhance the state of the field of management knowledge by integrating what is fragmented and evaluating what is contested. In this chapter we will first describe different types of publication. Second, we will offer guidelines for the execution of a literature review.

11.2 Types of publication

Scientific journals

Scientific journals are the most important medium for the publication of research results. Articles in scientific journals present findings at the frontiers of knowledge and are often characterized by a limited scope. Most journal articles have a similar structure. The introduction usually answers five questions: what is the subject of the article? Why is this subject important? What is already known about this subject? What is not yet known about it – what 'gap' exists in the literature? What have the authors done to fill that gap? After the introduction, research articles usually discuss successively the theoretical background, hypotheses (if any), research methods, results, conclusions and implications. Whereas the introduction and the theoretical background position the article in the existing literature, the latter sections contain the specific contribution of a research article.

Not all articles follow the above structure. In the field of management science, many articles are conceptual or theoretical in nature. These articles present new ideas, concepts, theoretical perspectives or hypotheses. Another type of article in scientific journals is the review article. A review article provides an overview of studies and research results within an area of inquiry. Such review articles are valuable introductions to the literature. Important references can be found in them, which are useful if one wants to explore the area further. An example of a research article in the field of innovation management is the overview of product development research by Brown and Eisenhardt (1995), published in the *Academy of Management Review*. The title of this article shows that it contains a literature review: 'Product development: past research, present findings, and future directions'.

Most scientific journals use a thorough selection procedure. Papers submitted to these journals will be *double blind refereed*. This means that the paper is sent to a number of reviewers who do not know who the author of the paper is, and the author does not know who the reviewers are. This double blind review procedure is intended to make the evaluation of submitted papers as objective as possible and to rule out preferential treatments and old-boy networks. When reviewers have read a paper thoroughly, they can reject the paper, accept the paper or ask for improvements before deciding on acceptance. Due to this procedure, scientific journals usually contain articles of high quality that make a clear contribution to the existing literature.

Of course, scientific journals differ in quality. Journals that employ higher selection norms usually publish better articles. Several ranking systems attempt to represent these quality differences. The most widely used ranking is based upon the 'impact score' of journals, which is an average of the amount of times articles in a journal are cited, traceable through the Social Science Citation Index (SSCI). It is important to be aware of these quality differences and pay particular attention to articles in the top journals (though these are sometimes more difficult to read and less practitioner-oriented). Leading journals in the field of management science are *Academy of Management Journal, Academy of Management Review, Administrative Science Quarterly, Management Science, Organization Science, Organization Studies, Journal of Management Studies* and *Strategic Management Journal*. These journals have a relatively broad scope. There are also many top quality journals that have a more limited focus. Examples are *Journal of Marketing, Journal of Product Innovation Management, R&D Management, MIS Quarterly, European Journal of Operational Research, International Journal of Operations and Production Management, Organizational Behavior and Human Decision Processes*.

Professional journals

In addition to scientific journals, one can also find professional journals in the library. These journals are targeted at an audience of practitioners, including managers and consultants. The most popular professional journals include *Harvard Business Review, MIT Sloan Management Review*, and *California Management Review*. Professional journals have a pragmatic instead of a theoretical focus. These journals seldom publish original research – only popularized versions of research published elsewhere. In addition, they publish case studies and experiences of managers and consultants and provide space for more speculative theorizing. In general, ideas presented in professional journals are far less substantiated by arguments and empirical research than articles in scientific journals. Professional journals can be a rich source of innovative ideas and solution concepts for BPS projects, but one cannot rely blindly on the ideas presented.

Books

If you compare books within the field of management science, you'll notice that there are several types of them. For our present purposes it suffices to distinguish between *management books, scholarly books, textbooks* and *handbooks*. These types of books differ in their value for BPS projects.

Management books are the book-length equivalent of articles in professional journals such as *Harvard Business Review*. Management books are often based on a mix of the author's own experiences, theories of others, and speculation. Management books are particularly oriented at the design, change and improvement of organizations. This makes them suited as a source of ideas for redesign. But take care – although the ideas presented may be appealing, they are seldom tested (do not consider one or two success stories to be a serious test), and frequently packaged in propagandistic language.

Scholarly books present the outcomes of research programs or several individual studies. For example, *The Innovation Journey* (Van de Ven *et al* 1999) presents results of the Minnesota Innovation Research Program, which lasted for more than fifteen years. Frequently, parts of the results of such a research program have been published before in scientific journals. Another type of scientific book is the edited volume. An edited volume contains a set of scientific articles from different authors, brought together and edited by one or a few of these authors.

Finally, the library contains handbooks and textbooks. Examples of handbooks are the *Handbook of Industrial Engineering* (Salvendy 2001) and *The Oxford Handbook of Organization Theory* (Tsoukas and Knudsen 2003). Both handbooks and textbooks provide an overview of a certain field of study and summarize years of scientific research. Whereas textbooks are usually written for students and guide newcomers into a subject, handbooks usually do not have this educational orientation. Textbooks and handbooks are excellent starting points in the quest for useful literature since they summarize and integrate existing concepts, theories and empirical findings. Unfortunately, it often takes many years before handbooks and textbooks about a new field of study are published.

Quick reference materials (encyclopaedias and dictionaries)

Most people associate encyclopaedias with collections of general facts about countries, famous people, history and so on. However, many scientific specialties, especially those with a long history, have their own encyclopaedias. For example, philosophers created the ten-volume *Routledge Encyclopaedia of Philosophy* (Craig 1998). Within the fields of business and management there are also general and more specialized encyclopaedias available. Examples are the *International Encyclopaedia of Business and Management* (Warner 1996) and the *Encyclopaedia of Operations Research and Management Science* (Gass and Harris 2001). In addition to encyclopaedias, many fields of study have their own dictionaries, in which the important concepts used in that field are explained. An example is *A Dictionary of Human Resource Management* (Heery and Noon 2001).

Encyclopaedias can be a good starting point for a literature study. Relevant entries in an encyclopaedia sketch the main ideas and findings concerning a topic and point to key publications. However, the quality of encyclopaedias varies. Therefore, the use of multiple encyclopaedias (if available) provides a more reliable overview of a topic. For the key areas of a study, encyclopaedias will provide too little information but will be a useful starting point. For a quick introduction or explanation of a concept, an encyclopaedia can be sufficient. For example, if students want to learn something about human memory, they may check out the *Encyclopaedia of Psychology* (Kazdin 2000). Finally, we want to mention the *Sage Encyclopaedia of Social Science Research Methods* (Lewis-Beck *et al* 2004) as a collection of introductions to many methodological issues.

Other types of research publications

Besides scientific journals and books, there are several other types of publications in which results of scientific research are published. First, *conference proceedings* contain papers that have been presented at a particular conference. Conference proceedings are particularly valuable for finding out the latest research. Frequently, improved drafts of these papers are later submitted to journals. Most libraries have only the proceedings of the most important conferences available. Second, many research institutes publish series of working papers. These papers describe research-in-progress, and later versions are often submitted to journals. Therefore, these are also particularly important to find out about recently finished and current research projects. Third, research done by students is published in theses and dissertations. Finally, there is so-called *grey literature*. This is literature that is written for a restricted audience and is difficult to identify and obtain (Hart 2001). An example is a report written for a company and declared 'confidential'.

11.3 Focusing a literature review

In order to use relevant scientific knowledge, it has to be extracted from the immense amount of literature available. This is done in a literature review. The remainder of this chapter presents guidelines for a good literature review. A basic rule for a good literature review is that the same attention is paid to quality as is done in empirical research.

Basing the use of existing literature on a systematic review contrasts with the opportunistic use of literature. Frequently, claims in publications are backed up by one or a few references, although there is a lot more literature on the topic. In the best cases, the cited work integrates the existing literature in a valid way. However, publications are also cited for opportunistic reasons: these are the only publications the author knows on the subject or these publications fit the ideas of the author. To make things worse, many references are 'empty'. *Empty references* are references to publications that do not contain any original evidence for the phenomenon under investigation, but only refer to other studies to substantiate their claim (Harzing 2002). Empty referencing is risky, since the citing work may have interpreted the cited work in a special or erroneous way, or the cited work may not provide any evidence either. This threat is multiplied when empty references cite empty references in turn. Harzing (2002) showed how such chains and networks of empty referencing create a pretence of validity, but actually undermine the credibility of scientific research.

Of course, students need to balance the time spent on a literature search and the time spent on other activities. Even for full-time researchers it is impossible to perform a systematic literature review on every relevant aspect of their study. However, for the central topics of a study, a systematic review will be valuable.

Before one commences a survey of the existing literature, one needs to know what to learn from it. We distinguish three different objectives that a literature search in a BPS project may have.

First, students may want to *familiarize* themselves with a topic. Find out what the most important questions, concepts, models, theories and methods are. This provides the basis for naming and framing. One frequently practiced approach to familiarize oneself is to pick the books and articles that one first stumbles upon. However, this is not the most efficient approach and easily leads to a biased perspective. It is more efficient and reliable to use literature that presents an overview: review articles, encyclopaedias, textbooks and handbooks. After students have familiarized themselves with a topic, they are better able to formulate more specific questions for a literature review. If they fail to do so, their search will be undirected and the outcomes of their literature survey will be fragmented.

Second, students may want to *explore* the literature for something they are interested in. In order to develop directions for redesign, for example, they may be interested in solution concepts that are described in the literature. Furthermore, the literature can be explored for definitions, theoretical models, causes, measurement instruments, advantages and disadvantages of an approach, and so on.

Third, literature may be searched for evidence in favour and against a solution concept or hypothesis. This objective of a literature review has been emphasized by authors pleading for an evidence-based or evidence-informed approach to professional practice (Tranfield *et al* 2003; Pawson 2002a). Imagine that you came across brainstorming as a solution concept for improved organizational creativity. However, if an author claims that it will work, this does not guarantee that it will work. Even if an author presents supporting evidence, it is wise to search for criticism and contradictory findings. Therefore it is preferable to gather the evidence concerning the effect of brainstorming on creativity. In theory-oriented projects one may be interested in the evaluation of evidence supporting and contradicting a particular hypothesis or theory.

Whatever it is that you are looking for, be sure that you make clear what it is. Explicate your goals as clearly as possible. Determine the relevant key words. List the questions that you want to answer. Make a graphic representation, if possible. Yet, searching and using literature is often an iterative process. Reading literature helps to name and frame a problem, which in turn helps to formulate the goals of a literature search. A basic level of understanding is needed to know what one does not yet know (Miyake and Norman 1979). It is a characteristic of literature reviews in management science that questions change and become more detailed during the course of a literature survey (Tranfield *et al* 2003).

11.4 Searching literature

The best way to become familiar with a topic and to gain insight into the theories, methods, findings and debates, is to read reviews and overviews of the literature on a topic. Particularly suited are review articles, entries in encyclopaedias and (chapters and sections in) textbooks and handbooks. It saves a lot of work if one or more of these are found on the topic of study. Since these types of publication contain many relevant references, they will facilitate the quest for more detailed literature.

Searching literature in a systematic way increases the chance that much of the relevant literature is found, reduces the probability of a biased review, and increases the reproducibility of a literature search. A systematic search process therefore enhances the quality of a review. Systematic reviews may also be of use for others: they counter the fragmented and contested state of management science. Below we will describe search strategies that enable a systematic search process. However, if you execute a literature review, you'll also discover the value of serendipity. Serendipity refers to the discovery of things that were not looked for. It often occurs that one finds relevant literature in a place where one was not searching for it.

This section presents three ways to search systematically for literature (see also Hart 2001): (1) search engines; (2) the 'snowball' method; (3) scanning library sections and journals.

Search engines

The first option of where to search for literature is to use search engines. There are several types of search engine available, providing entries to different types of publications:

(a) *Library catalogues*

Each library has its own catalogue. Most of them are available online. The catalogue of a library usually refers to books, reports, encyclopaedias and journals held within that library, but not to articles within those journals. Most search engines of catalogues enable one to search by title word, author and a few other criteria. Since many catalogues are public and can be accessed online, the catalogues of many libraries can be searched. In addition to catalogues of single libraries, there are also combined catalogues available, like national catalogues.

(b) *Indexes and abstracts databases*

For many subjects there are electronic databases available that contain references to (predominantly) journal articles. The database called *ABI/Inform* is most important for management science. ABI/Inform contains abstracts of articles from approximately 1,000 business and management journals in the English language. Among other options,

ABI/Inform makes it possible to select articles by title word, author, time of publication, journal title, and words in the abstract. The latter option in particular increases the probability of finding relevant articles. In addition to ABI/Inform, other indexing and abstracts databases may be used, such as *EconLit* for economic literature and *PsycINFO* for psychological literature.

(c) *Citation indexes*

A search technique that is not often used, but may be highly valuable for a systematic search of the literature, is searching for articles that cite a target publication. This way of searching is enabled by the SSCI, which can be accessed through the *Web of Science*. If one knows a key publication on a topic, one may use the SSCI to find later articles that refer to that key publication. This helps to find a large share of the literature on a topic, since scientific articles usually cite the key publications on the same topic. An alternative to the SSCI is *NEC CiteSeer* (www.citeseer.nj.nec.com/cs). This search engine looks for citations in reports available at the internet.

(d) *Search engines on the internet*

Many students look for publications on the internet, and use the common search engines to do so (such as Google). However, the internet is not the best place to find scholarly literature. Contrary to what some people expect, the content of scientific journals is not publicly available on the internet. At best, one finds research reports not (yet) published in journals. It is more likely that one finds all kind of documents which have not been checked for quality by peer researchers and editors. This may be useful for a first impression, but students can better spend their time searching for and reading literature using other methods.

The 'snowball' method

A second way to search literature is to trace references. Encyclopaedias, text-books, handbooks and review articles are an especially important source of references to relevant literature. If overviews of the literature are not to hand, they can be traced using the search engines listed above. Relevant articles in top journals are also a good place to start. These articles usually refer to the important articles on the topic that were published earlier. Searching via references is sometimes called the 'snowball-method': a reference in one article points to other articles; references in those articles point to an even wider set of articles; and so on. The set of relevant articles expands just like a snowball gets thicker and thicker.

Scanning library sections and journals

A third systematic way to search relevant literature is to scan shelves with books or volumes of journals. This strategy is particularly suited for familiarizing oneself with a particular topic. For example, one may scan the last two years of the two most relevant journals. One can also scan the shelves of books with a particular library code. If one is searching for information on a specific topic, the contents page of books can also be used to find out whether it contains relevant information.

Queries in databases frequently yield a large amount of 'hits'. Likewise, the snowball method and the scanning method can yield a large amount of potentially relevant publications (see below). However, time constraints limit the amount of publications that can be read. Therefore it is wise to select among hits on the basis of relevancy and quality. For example, only those articles that were published in peer-reviewed scientific journals, or only in the top scientific journals, may be selected. Or, if evidence is collected with regard to a hypothesis, theory or method, only those articles that present empirical studies may be selected.

A literature review should be executed with the same attention to quality as an empirical research project. In Chapter 12 we discuss controllability as a necessary prerequisite for the evaluation of research products. The same holds for literature reviews. A good literature review describes the ways in which publications were sourced and selected, so that others are put in position to replicate it. As a consequence, others will not replicate it, but will trust the results of a controllable literature review.

11.5 Integrating ideas and findings

After one has found and selected literature on a topic, the content of this literature has to be interpreted and combined. Again we distinguish different ways in which this can be approached.

Sequential presentation

This approach consists of a sequential treatment of publications and the ideas and findings presented in them. This is the type of review students are inclined to write. It shows what other researchers have said and done, but it does not add anything. It leaves the literature as fragmented as it was. This approach may fit the goal of familiarizing oneself with a scientific field, but a review has more value if ideas and findings from the selected publications are integrated.

Qualitative integration

To provide added value to the existing literature, a literature review should go beyond sequentially presenting ideas and findings and integrate them. The integration of findings can be done both qualitatively and quantitatively. The quantitative integration of research findings is suited for the integration of evidence concerning a well-defined hypothesis. The qualitative integration of findings has more applications. However, there are far fewer procedures available in the literature.

A general approach that helps to get from a sequential review of publications to a qualitative integration is by means of a matrix. First, create rows for publications and columns for topics or factors that one is interested in. Second, fill the cells of the matrix with the findings or claims of each article with regard to each of the topics listed in the columns. Third, rotate the matrix (actually or imaginarily), so that the focus shifts from the publications to the topics, and combine the findings or claims of different publications about each of the topics into a coherent story.

The following tactics may be of additional help in the process of integrating findings:

– *compare*; for example, compare what is the same in a set of definitions you found in the literature and what is different; or compare the phases that are defined in different phase models of decision-making. Comparison shows the differences and similarities between definitions, models, and so on, and provides the basis for choosing among them;

– *make distinctions*; for example, many literature reviews distinguish different streams in the literature; the student may also distinguish different approaches to solve a problem, arguments for and against something, different situations, and so on;

– *make lists*; for example, if one explores the literature for factors influencing performance on a particular parameter, the literature can be integrated by making a list of these factors. Similarly, lists can be made of solution concepts, models, properties, arguments, evidence, instruments, guidelines, definitions, effects, criteria, and so on;

– *construct matrices that relate lists or dimensions*; for example, in a project at Rolls-Royce, a student explored the literature for measuring instruments and used a matrix to characterize each of them on a number of dimensions. This enabled the evaluation of the suitability of these measurement instruments. Likewise a matrix can be used to represent solution concepts and their advantages and disadvantages, and so on;

- *theorize*; each of the activities above is a contribution to the development of an integrated theory on a subject. This is the ultimate goal of a qualitative research review. For example, by comparing published case studies you may develop a theory on what solution concept works in what situation (specify technological rules). Pawson (2002a; 2002b) presents an elaborated approach for the qualitative synthesis of research that aims at the development of such a pragmatic theory.

Quantitative integration (meta-analysis)

Over the past decades a range of quantitative approaches to the integration of research findings has been developed. The quantitative synthesis of the results of separate studies is called *meta-analysis*. The basic idea behind meta-analysis is that results of individual studies are used as data points in a statistical analysis. The quantitative integration of findings is more sensitive than the qualitative inspection for patterns that exist within the findings of studies (Light and Pillemer 1984). Several meta-analytical techniques exist (see Cooper 1998; Cooper and Hedges 1993). The easiest approach to meta-analysis is the *vote count* method. One may count the number of studies that support a hypothesis and compare that with the number of studies that do not support it. A more sophisticated technique is the combination of probabilities. Quantitative studies reject or accept a hypothesis based on the probability that a result is produced by chance. A combination of these probabilities yields far more reliable results than any single study can. Quantitative techniques can also be used to estimate the *effect size*, that is, the strength of a relationship. Finally, quantitative techniques can be used to determine the cause of varying results and contradictory findings.

12 Quality criteria for research

12.1 Introduction

One of the central operational goals of production processes is to meet the quality criteria for the goods produced. These criteria pertain, for example, to a product's strength, functioning or resistance to wear. If a product does not meet its associated quality criteria, it loses much of its value. The same holds for business problem-solving (BPS) projects. Executing a BPS project can also be interpreted as a production process. The deliverables of this production process are defined in the assignment (see Chapter 5.6). This chapter discusses quality criteria for the products of a BPS project.

BPS projects can be evaluated on several criteria. We make a distinction between research-oriented criteria and change-oriented criteria. Research-oriented criteria relate to the research aspects of BPS projects. They are particularly relevant for diagnosis and evaluation, since these comprise most research activities. Research-oriented criteria are less important during problem definition, redesign and implementation. Change-oriented criteria, including relevancy and the creation of support, are more relevant for those latter activities. Change-oriented criteria are discussed in Chapter 2. The present chapter will only deal with research-oriented criteria.

Many people say that the ultimate aim of research is to yield true conclusions (Goldman 1999). However, others doubt whether truth is a useful concept, or quarrel about the meaning of truth (Lawson and Appignanesi 1989). Anyway, given the fallibility of our knowledge, we can never be sure whether a conclusion is true or not. However, though the objective determination of truth and falsity is unattainable, reverting to subjective opinions is undesirable. We can do better than that. Many authors acknowledge that the central aim of research is to strive after inter-subjective agreement (Habermas 1981; Swanborn 1996). Inter-subjective agreement refers to consensus between the actors who deal with a research problem. In BPS projects inter-subjective agreement is something to strive after. For example, inter-subjective agreement on a diagnosis is important to get support for a solution.

The most important research-oriented quality criteria are controllability, reliability and validity (Swanborn 1996; Yin 1994). These are important because they provide the basis for inter-subjective agreement on research results. Sociological studies of the production of scientific knowledge (Latour 1987) and organizational knowledge (Gherardi and Nicolini 2001) emphasize that social factors, like power, also have a decisive influence on the development of inter-subjective agreeement. Nevertheless, in theory-based BPS the analyzes should meet the quality criteria. Controllability, reliability and validity pertain to research outcomes, claims about reality that are based upon research. They apply to measurements, explanations, conclusions, interpretations, causal models, and so on. For example:
– 'production loss is fourteen per cent';
– 'long lead times are caused by high production losses';
– 'the management of this company is a late adopter of new concepts like e-commerce since it prefers to work with "proven technology"'.
These claims can be said to be controllable, reliable and valid, or not. The concepts of reliability and validity can also be applied to the process of research and research instruments. Stating that a research process or a research instrument is reliable or valid means that it is able to yield reliable or valid results. The more research meets these criteria, the less reason there is to question its results.

Quality criteria for research can be used in two ways. In the first place, the criteria can be used to manage the quality of one's own research. When students develop a research design or choose data collection techniques and methods for analysis, they should reflect upon the quality of the results that their choices will bring. Based upon such an assessment, you can either choose to follow your plans or change them. Therefore we will not only discuss the criteria and how they can be assessed, but also pay attention to ways to improve on each of the criteria.

In the second place, quality criteria can be used to evaluate research done by others. BPS projects benefit from the application of existing theories. As most topics of problem-solving have already received much attention in the literature, a literature search usually yields lots of books, journal articles, reports and internet sites that seem to be relevant. However, the fact that something has been written down and published does not guarantee that it is of sufficient quality. Therefore it is necessary to assess the quality of available literature. That is where the quality criteria presented in this chapter come in.

Furthermore, the quality criteria for research can be used by the principal client and the steering committee to appraise the BPS project that is done for them. If students execute a project within an organization of professionals, they will be frequently called upon to justify their claims. To facilitate the appraisal by the client organization, and to convince them of the quality of work, it is recommendable to discuss quality criteria in the reports and presentations on the project. Explicit attention to quality criteria also forces students to reflect on the ways in which their projects deal with those criteria.

In the following sections we discuss controllability, reliability and validity. Both reliability and validity are subdivided into different types. These discussions are based primarily upon the use of these concepts in traditional theory-oriented research. However, where necessary we adapt the meaning of particular criteria for application in BPS projects. Finally, we will also discuss the importance of the recognition of research results.

12.2 Controllability

Controllability is the first requirement for reaching inter-subjective agreement on research results. Controllability is a prerequisite for the evaluation of validity and reliability. In order to make research results controllable, researchers have to reveal how they executed a study: how were data collected? How were respondents selected? What questions were asked? Under what circumstances was the study executed? How were data analyzed? How were conclusions drawn? The detailed description of a study enables others to replicate it, so that they can check whether they get the same outcomes. It is more likely, though, that others will not replicate it, but use the description to judge the reliability and validity of the study.

Scholarly articles usually address questions like the ones above in a methodological section. It is advisable to follow that example in the report of a BPS project. As a rule of thumb a study should be described in such a way that somebody else is able to replicate it. Students can anticipate the future presentation of their research process by writing memos about their research activities (Strauss and Corbin 1998). These memos and other materials that document the research process are additional means for the evaluation of research.

In addition to a detailed description of research methods, controllability also requires that results are presented as precisely as possible (Swanborn 1996). Take for example the conclusion that 'there is some degree of dissatisfaction among the employees'. More information is needed to evaluate that statement: where are they dissatisfied about? How dissatisfied are they? Does that hold for all employees? Without an answer to these questions, without a precise statement of the conclusion, it is impossible to verify or falsify it.

12.3 Reliability

Reliability is a concept that seems to be easy to grasp but nevertheless difficult to define. In general, we call something unreliable when we cannot depend upon it, when we cannot trust it. A car that occasionally fails to start is unreliable. A person who does not keep his promises is unreliable. The general association of reliability with dependability and trustworthiness holds for research as well, but it has a more specific interpretation.

The results of a study are reliable when they are independent of the particular characteristics of that study and can therefore be replicated in other studies (Yin 1994; Swanborn 1996). The methodological literature recognizes four potential sources of bias: the researcher, the instrument, the respondents and the situation. Research results should be independent of the researcher who conducted the study, the respondents, the measuring instrument employed and the specific situation in which the study was carried out (Cook and Campbell 1979: 43–44; Cooper and Schindler 2003; 229–230; Swanborn 1996). In other words, a repetition of the study by another researcher, with a different research instrument, with different respondents or in another situation, should yield the same results. When research results cannot be replicated, there is little basis for inter-subjective agreement.

A common strategy to determine the reliability of a measurement is to repeat it. By repeating a measurement, one can determine to what degree measurement results differ from each other. If there is no difference, the research results seem to be independent of the specific characteristics of both studies. Repeating a measurement has at the same time the advantage that measurements can be combined in order to increase reliability. Combining measurements may consist of calculating the mean of a series of values, but it may also consist of an attempt to reach consensus on the interpretation of qualitative data. It is better to take average of several imperfectly reliable results than to trust one of them, since the average is less dependent on the specific characteristics of one of the studies. Doing more measurements is therefore another common strategy to improve reliability. This will be elaborated in the following discussion of different types of reliability.

Researchers and reliability

Research results are (more) reliable when they are independent of the person who has conducted the study. Sometimes it makes a big difference who observes, interviews, concludes or performs any other research activity. Goldman (1999: 230) makes a distinction between *hot biases* and *cold biases*. Hot biases refer to the influence of interests, motivations and emotions of researchers on their results. For example, researchers may be tempted to shape conclusions to please financial sponsors. Cold biases refer to subjective influences of the researcher that have a cognitive origin and no personal motivation. One example of a cold bias is confirmation bias: people have a tendency to pay more attention to evidence that confirms their beliefs than to evidence that contradicts their beliefs. People have a tendency to interpret observations in such a way that they are in accordance with their beliefs (Weick 1995). Both hot biases and cold biases harm reliability.

Some instruments of data collection and analysis leave more room for biases than others. For example, interviews depend more upon the personal characteristics of the interviewer than a written survey does. The smaller the possible influence of a researcher, the more objective the results are.

Whether research results are independent of the person conducting a study can be assessed by having somebody else repeat the study. When objects or events are coded (see Chapter 10), it is common to have two people do the coding. Reliability can be assessed by determining the correlation between the codes assigned by both researchers. This is called the *inter-rater reliability*. When the inter-rater reliability is high, both researchers' codes are alike and it is possible to trust each coder's results. If inter-rater reliability is low, the coding procedure may need to be improved. If this is not possible, different researchers need to average their codes or come to a consensus. Of course, there are practical limitations to the repetition of research by others. The rate of change in organizations makes replication of research in BPS projects difficult. Moreover, BPS projects are intended to contribute to organizational change processes.

There are several ways to increase reliability through an improvement of researcher independency of results (Swanborn 1996: 24–26). Above we discussed the value of using multiple researchers and working towards consensus or using average results. Another strategy is *standardization*. Standardization is the development and use of explicit procedures for data collection, analysis and interpretation. An example is to choose structured interviews instead of open interviews. Another example is the development of a case-study protocol, which guides the execution of a case study (Yin 1994). The more procedures have been fixed in advance, the less the personal characteristics of a researcher can influence results. However, research practices can never be captured fully in explicit procedures. Research, as well as other human practices, ultimately rests on a basis of tacit knowing (Polanyi 1958). Finally, the use of tools can reduce dependency on a researcher. Think for example of the use of electronic sensors used in tennis to detect whether a serve is in or out. For qualitative analyses (see Chapter 10), several software packages have been developed that help a researcher to work systematically. Examples are *Atlas.ti*, *NVIVO* and *The Ethnograph*.

Instruments and reliability

Frequently there are several instruments or techniques available for studying the same phenomenon. It is not uncommon for different instruments to yield diverging results. However, research results should be independent of the specific instruments used. Outcomes should be replicable with other instruments. This holds for different copies of the same instrument. For example, if you weigh yourself on a pair of scales, you expect it to give the same weight as another pair of scales.

If different research strategies are used for studying the same phenomenon, the results of these different strategies should be in line. If one gets different results, these may be both *complementary* and *contradictory*. For example, surveys and interviews have different advantages. Combining them may therefore yield complementary results. However, they may also yield contradictory results. For example, what people say (their 'espoused theories') often differs from what they do (their 'theories-in-use'). Therefore, observation and interviewing may yield contradictory results. In those cases in which different research instruments are likely to yield complementary or contradictory results, using only one instrument would yield unreliable results. Reliability is served by using a multiple research instruments. This approach is often called *triangulation* (Yin 1994: 92). Triangulation is the combination of multiple sources of evidence and it is well suited for use in BPS projects. This may be a combination of interviews, documents, archives, observation, surveys and other instruments. Triangulation can remedy the specific shortcomings and biases of these instruments by complementing and correcting each other.

Reliability concerning instruments also plays within instruments. Different questions or items within an interview or survey can also be considered as different instruments (Swanborn 1996). Questionnaires typically contain a set of items to measure a particular variable. Each of these items intends to measure the same variable, but uses different wording and focuses on different aspects. Such a set of items, which is combined to a single score, is known as a Likert scale. Based on the statistical correlation of items it is possible to determine the degree to which different items replicate each other's findings. A common measure for this is Cronbach's Alpha. If Cronbach's Alpha is sufficiently high, the Likert scale is a reliable measuring instrument. Given that it is often difficult to develop reliable scales, it is beneficial to use reliable scales that are already published instead of developing one's own scales.

Respondents and reliability

Many students are surprised to learn that different people within a company have widely diverging opinions. Though this may seem troublesome at first sight, it is inevitable. People have their own perspective, their own view on reality. Different people have different conceptual schemes, different values, different observations and draw different conclusions. Some studies are purposefully designed to learn about the details of the perspective of one person or a group of people (for example Walsh 1995). At other times the perspectives of organization members are not an object of study in their own right but a source of information about organizational reality. In that case you want the information you get to correspond to reality, or at least, to get an inter-subjective view by combining perspectives.

Research results should be independent of the respondents included in the study. Most studies select respondents – the people who participate in the study – out of a larger group. In quantitative studies, the respondents selected are often called *the sample* and the larger group from which they are selected *the population*. When only a portion of the potential respondents is asked for an interview, a survey or an experiment, the question arises whether other respondents would have provided the same answers as the chosen respondents. When selecting respondents, you should ask yourself whether the choice for particular organization members as respondents might influence the results of the study. Do these respondents offer an objective view or balanced mixture of perspectives? Research results become unreliable when the selection of respondents leads to results that differ to a substantial degree from the results that would be obtained with other respondents.

Take the following example. A group of researchers studying the role of project leaders in a new business creation only interviewed a number of those project leaders. One of the conclusions of the study was that project leaders were of crucial importance to the success of new business creation projects and should be given a high degree of autonomy. However, other organization members would probably have told another story. Including the views of project team members and top management would have yielded a more balanced conclusion regarding the role of project leaders. Thus, this is an example of a study that is unreliable due to the choice of respondents.

Three principles should be followed to counter this source of unreliability. First, as many as possible of the roles, departments, groups and so on. who are involved in the problem area, need to be *represented* among the respondents. In the above-mentioned study, reliability could have been improved by interviewing project team members, top management and other organization members as well. Second, if the group of potential respondents is large and if you are not interested in differences within that group, it is appropriate to select respondents at random, to create a select sample. If everybody has the same chance of being selected, and if a sufficient number of respondents is chosen, chances are low that the particular sample will yield a distorted picture. You can learn much more about this in classical treatments of methodology and statistics (for example Cooper and Schindler 2003: 176–216). Third, the general strategy to increase reliability is to increase the number of respondents.

Circumstances and reliability

Differences between the circumstances under which a measurement can be executed are another source of unreliability. Early in the morning the interviewee may be in a different mood than in the afternoon, and may therefore give different answers in an interview. Also, an interviewee's stated opinion may be influenced by a recent negative experience. Or interviewees may not say something because others can hear them. These factors influence the results of an interview or a whole study. When the particular situation leads to results that cannot be replicated in other circumstances, research results are unreliable.

An obvious way to increase reliability concerning circumstances is to carry out a study at different moments in time. For BPS projects this comes naturally, since these projects require prolonged presence in an organization. The student will experience a multitude of circumstances, will become more and more of an insider, and will therefore be able to recognize what are unique and what are common circumstances.

12.4 Validity

Validity is the third major criterion for the evaluation of research results. The literature contains few general discussions of validity, but more discussions of specific types of validity. In general, we define validity by employing the epistemological notion of *justification* (Audi 1998): a research result is valid when it is justified by the way it is generated. The way it is generated should provide good reasons to believe that the research result is true or adequate. Thus, validity refers to the relationship between a research result or conclusion and the way it has been generated.

This definition of validity implies that validity presupposes reliability. If a measurement is not reliable, this limits our reasons to believe that the research results obtained with it are true. On the other hand, reliability does not presuppose validity. One can have a perfectly reliable measure, which does not yield valid research results.

The abstract definition of validity will become more comprehensible when we discuss different types of validity: construct validity, internal validity and external validity. We base our discussion of these criteria on Swanborn (1996) and Yin (1994). Other authors define concepts slightly differently (for example Cooper and Schindler 2003). The methodological literature discerns still some other types of validity, but those are less relevant for BPS projects.

Construct validity

Construct validity is the extent to which a measuring instrument measures what it is intended to measure (De Groot 1969). Thus, construct validity refers to the quality of the operationalization of a concept. Construct validity is high if the way a concept is measured corresponds to the meaning of that concept. For example, a measuring instrument that is intended to measure employee satisfaction, but only asks for the attitude of employees towards management, has a low construct validity.

There are two sides to construct validity: (1) the concept should be covered completely, and (2) the measurement should have no components that do not fit the meaning of the concept. The components of a measurement should be both adequate and complete. Within BPS projects construct validity should be interpreted broadly. It is not only relevant for quantitative measurements of properties, but also for qualitative data collection. In open interviews, for example, a concept can be covered completely or not.

There are at least three ways to assess construct validity. First, students can evaluate measuring instruments and data collection techniques by themselves. They may ask themselves whether the components of their measurement fit the meaning of the concept they intend to measure and whether the concept is completely covered. Second, they can ask experts to evaluate the measuring instrument. Third, they can determine the correlation of their operationalization with measurements of other concepts with which it should correlate, according to theory (Swanborn 1996: 23). If this association is not found, the construct validity of the measurement is dubitable (or the theory is not adequate).

Construct validity can be improved by repairing the flaws that were detected, either by including new components to a measurement or by deleting existing items. Sometimes triangulation can be valuable (Yin 1994). Above we explained that triangulation is the use of multiple research instruments in order to combine the results obtained with them. If one research instrument, such as a survey, is unable to cover all aspects of a concept, this lack of construct validity can be remedied by the use of an additional instrument.

Construct validity and reliability pose contradictory demands in some cases. Some instruments are more reliable, but have a lower construct validity. Others have a higher construct validity, but are less reliable. For example, the amount of knowledge created within an industrial research laboratory is often measured by the amount of patents generated. This is a highly reliable measurement. The amount of patents is a discrete and at any moment in time fixed number. However, the construct validity of this measurement is relatively low. Knowledge is broader than what is patented. Some new insights are not patented for strategic reasons and tacit knowledge cannot be patented at all. Another approach is to determine the amount of knowledge generated by a survey, observations or interviews. This may yield a more complete coverage of the concept and therefore a higher construct validity, but the reliability of those research instruments is lower. If reliability and validity contradict in this way, researchers have to decide which criterion they consider as the most important.

Internal validity

Construct validity concerns the measurement of phenomena. Internal validity concerns conclusions about the relationship between phenomena. The results of a study are internally valid when conclusions about relationships are justified and complete. Classical methodology has particularly focused on the adequacy of conclusions about causal relationships. A conclusion about a causal relationship is internally valid, when there are good reasons to assume that the proposed relationship is adequate. In order to establish the internal validity of a proposed relationship, one has to make sure that there are *no plausible competing explanations*. If a correlation is found between phenomenon A and phenomenon B, one may be tempted to conclude that A is a cause of B. However, correlation is a necessary, but not a sufficient condition for causality. It may also be the case that B is the cause of A, or that both A and B are caused by a third phenomenon, C. For example, if a correlation is found between driving a Mercedes and wearing a tie, it is not justified to conclude that driving a Mercedes causes somebody to wear a tie or vice versa. It is probably a third factor, someone's social economic position, which explains the correlation between these phenomena.

In the methodological approach of the regulative cycle, the concept of internal validity refers both to the adequacy and the completeness of suggested relationships. The diagnostic phase consists of the exploration and validation of a business problem and its causes. Internal validity is high when many of the actual causes of the business problem are found. Studying the problem area from multiple perspectives can facilitate the discovery of all causes. This is sometimes called *theoretical triangulation*: viewing a problem from several theoretical angles. A reflection on the problem mess discerned in the orientation will often suggest several potentially relevant theoretical perspectives. Business problems are usually not neatly in line with the academic division of labour. For example, problems in the field of logistics often benefit from employing the perspectives of quality management and organization theory as well. Yet, researchers and students sometimes tend to limit themselves to one perspective: their own preferred perspective. This increases the chance that important causes are overlooked and thus reduces internal validity.

In addition to the use of multiple perspectives, internal validity can be improved by systematic analysis. Both Chapter 6, on diagnosis, and Chapter 10, on qualitative research methods, discuss research strategies and tactics for developing an internally valid diagnosis. Chapter 9 discusses threats to internal validity in the evaluation step.

External validity

External validity refers to the *generalizability* of research results and conclusions to other people, organizations, countries, and situations. External validity is very important in theory-oriented research. Sometimes researchers are told that the use of only one case in research is insufficient, since it is impossible to draw general conclusions on the basis of a single case. How can it be guaranteed that what works in one organization also works in another organization? This questions the external validity of a study.

External validity is often less important in BPS projects, since these projects focus on one specific problem. Yet, sometimes a BPS project employs a pilot study, or is itself a pilot. In those cases it is necessary to assess whether the results from the pilot study can also be expected in other departments or organizations. The external validity of a study depends upon the differences between the studied department or organization and other departments or organizations. External validity can be increased by increasing the number of objects studied. Depending on the research approach, these extra objects can be selected either at random or on theoretical grounds.

12.5 Recognition of results

The last criterion that we discuss is less prominent in the traditional methodological literature, but is very important in applied research: the recognition of research results (Van Dijk *et al* 1991: 139). Recognizability refers to the degree to which the principal client, the problem owner and other organization members, recognize research results in BPS projects. This does not have to mean that they could have formulated the results in advance, but that the results sound reasonable, plausible or at least possible to them.

Some degree of recognition is of crucial importance for the successful implementation of organizational changes. If the principal and other organization members cannot make sense of the results, it is difficult to reach inter-subjective agreement about proposed changes. Of course, a change agent should not only strive for research results that are in line with the views of the principal client and other organization members. If that were the case, the study would have little informative value. A study should increase the self-knowledge of those involved. Moreover, adapting conclusions to the views of a client ruins one's professional integrity.

The recognition of results can be assessed by presenting (intermediate) results to those involved. This is called a *member check* in the methodological literature (Swanborn 1996), since it is a check with the members of a community. If a student presents results in a meeting, organization members can react immediately. Their responses can be used for sharpening results. But, of course, organization members' opinions should never be copied blindly.

The chance that organization members recognize the results of a study increases if they are involved in it, for example by being interviewed or by being part of the platform group or steering committee. Other ways to increase recognition is to use appealing examples and to use concepts that are understood by the organization members. Practitioners prefer a narrative or visual presentation of findings instead of a text-based presentation (Worren *et al* 2002). In general, you need to understand the insider's perspective, and therefore you need to become, to some degree, an insider yourself.

12.6 Concluding remarks

It is important to realize that a positive assessment of reliability and validity is not yet a guarantee for truth or adequacy. A positive assessment increases the probability that results are adequate, but scientific practice shows many examples of apparently reliable and valid studies that contradict each other. Even when the business problem has been studied from several perspectives, important causes may still be overlooked. Conclusions about reliability and validity can always be questioned again based upon new insights.

Controllability, validity and reliability are the standard criteria that are discussed in most treatises on methodology for the social sciences. However, some social scientists do not consider these criteria to be very important or do not accept them at all. The last two decades have witnessed a number of alternative conceptions of quality criteria, based upon different social science paradigms (such as social constructivism and post-modernism). These social scientists consider traditional criteria to be part of a positivistic perspective, unsuited for the study of social phenomena (Guba and Lincoln 1989). One of the differences between natural sciences and the social sciences is that there exists a social relationship between the objects of social inquiry and the researchers studying them. According to Guba and Lincoln (1989) and others, quality criteria should pay more attention to this social context. An example of an alternative criterion they propose is *fairness*. Fairness refers to the degree to which the perspectives and values of different parties are acknowledged. Another criterion proposed by Guba and Lincoln (1989) is *educational authenticity*, which refers to the degree to which research contributes to the mutual understanding people have of each others' 'world'.

Part IV

Conclusion

In this final chapter we review the objectives of this handbook, its application domain and target group. We conclude by summarizing the benefits of including business problem-solving in a business course program.

13 Concluding remarks

In this handbook we have presented a design-focused and theory-based methodology for business problem-solving (BPS). Design-focused means that the primary aim of a BPS project is not generating knowledge and writing a smart report, but designing solutions to business problems (plus the accompanying change plans) to eventually improve performance of a certain business system. Even if the student is only involved in the design phase of a BPS project, the eventual performance improvement is the focus of the project. Theory-based means that in problem-solving the student does not rely solely on experience and informed common sense, but also state-of-the-art object and process knowledge.

The methodology presented in this handbook belongs to the family of rational problem-solving approaches; it is content-focused as opposed to process-focused. The student plays an expert role, rather than a coaching one. (One of the reasons for the choice of an expert role is that the BPS project is a learning experience in applying management theory in practice). At the same time the methodology takes into account that performance improvement involves organizational change and that organizational change does not only need technical interventions like a good report or presentation, but political and cultural interventions as well [Tichy 1983]. Therefore we pay attention to problem analysis, problem diagnosis and solution design as well as to change planning and developing support in the client organization for the solution and change plan. Students should not play pure expert roles, making analyses and designs independently. Rather they should operate in constant interaction with the client organization, testing results and developing organizational support for their solutions.

The methodology described in this book is basically a design approach, as opposed to a development approach to BPS (see Chapter 3.3). However, one can also use elements of a development approach, for example by first using a pilot implementation followed by a full-scale implementation on the basis of what has been learned from the pilot.

The methodology given in this handbook can be seen as a *technological rule* (Van Aken 2004), on the basis of a design-focused and theory-based approach. Like every technological rule, it is mid-range theory, that is, it has a certain application domain, the kind of business problems for which it is a promising approach. As discussed in Chapter 3.4, the problem should have a significant technical-economic component, but limited political and cultural components. Otherwise one might prefer more developing or facilitating approaches.

Rigorous use of a methodology means contextualization and justification. Copying a standard methodology for a specific problem is not rigorous use: it should be contextualized and adapted to the demands of the specific situation. However, rigorous use also means that every deviation from the standard methodology should be justifiable on the grounds of the demands of the situation, or on the grounds of recognized general limitations of the standard methodology.

The above also means that the methodology for business problem-solving, discussed in this handbook, should not be used as a protocol to be followed unquestioningly. It is also a 'natural' approach to problem-solving, not involving very specific steps or methods. It is, in fact, similar to the approach of many books on problem-solving or consulting, mentioned in Chapter 3.3. The differences are to be found in the special attention given to certain issues, such as the design of a sound overall approach to the BPS project, the use of theory, the discussions on designs, designing and social system design, the focus on eventual performance improvement instead of focusing on a smart solution or a nice report, and the importance of change planning and developing organizational support for the solution.

The primary target audience for this handbook consists of university business students, wanting to develop their business problem-solving skills in real-life settings. That implies that we choose the perspective of the involved outsider to the setting of the organizational problem and not the one of an organization member or of a manager. Managers play a different role in business problem-solving. They have responsibility for results and thus have to continuously monitor results and operations, and use continuous interventions to keep these operations under control. They can do so directly or through a coaching role by stimulating the self control of their subordinates. Managers usually have the power to implement designed improvements themselves, even if they too have to work on the creation of organizational support for them. The situation for outside problem-solvers is different. Instead of continuous monitoring and correcting, they have a project to run. They have to convince a principal (and other stakeholders) that their solution is a sound one and that it is advantageous to implement it. In our methodology they cannot fall back on a coaching role, leaving it to others to design solutions, but they have to play an active role in solution design.

The core competence of any professional is field problem-solving. If a business school is to be regarded as a Professional School, the development of business problem-solving competences should be its primary objective. These competences can be easily developed within the framework of one or more disciplinary courses. A more powerful way to develop these competences is to introduce a significant BPS project as the graduation assignment for the course program. Such a project can be seen as the grand finale of the program, as not only does it develop the core competences of the student, but it also creates a fine opportunity to apply the theory from the various disciplinary courses. Typically a project is carried out in a certain department of a company, so the discipline of this department tends to be the focus of the project. Nevertheless, a project also needs organization theory on structure, change and strategy (what is the importance of this problem for the department or company strategy?) Furthermore the student, as an involved outsider, often functions as a window to the outside, and will use information from adjoining departments, adjoining disciplines, or from outside the company. During the course of a BPS project the student has to draw together virtually everything that has been learnt on the program. In our experience we have often seen students develop from clumsy, ugly ducklings to confident, competent swans. We are sure that even without this unique learning experience most business graduates would develop into swans during their first years in business. But developing problem-solving skills in practice is very different from doing so in an academic context. All too often problem-solving in practice regresses to simply relying on experience and informed common sense. Learning theory-based business problem-solving is best done in the context of an academic course program under academic supervision.

This design-focused and theory-based methodology for business problem-solving has been developed on the basis of more than ten years' experience of supervising student BPS projects of the Techno-MBA-course program at Eindhoven University of Technology. In these projects our methodology has proven its value.

References

Ackoff, R. L. 1981a. 'The art and science of mess management', *Interfaces*, 11: 20–6

Ackoff, R. L. 1981b. *Creating the Corporate Future: Plan or Be Planned For.* New York: Wiley

Ackoff, R. L. and Vergara, E. 1981. 'Creativity in problem solving and planning: a review', *European Journal of Operational Research*, 7: 1–13

Ader, H. J. and Mellenbergh, G. 1999. *Research Methodology in the Social, Behavioral and Life Sciences.* London: Sage

Albert, K. J. (ed.) 1980. *Handbook of BPS.* New York: McGraw Hill

Argyris, C. 1993. *Knowledge for Action: a Guide for Overcoming Barriers to Organizational Change.* San Francisco: Jossey-Bass Publishers

Argyris, C. and Schön, D. A. 1978. *Organizational Learning: a Theory of Action Perspective.* Amsterdam: Addison-Wesley Publishers

Argyris, C., Putnam, R. and McLain Smith, D. 1985. *Action Science, Concepts, Methods, and Skills for Research and Intervention.* San Francisco: Jossey-Bass Publishers

Ashby, W. R. 1956. *An Introduction to Cybernetics.* London: Chapman and Hall

Audi, R. 1998. *Epistemology.* London: Routledge

Balogun, J. and Johnson, G. 2005. 'From intended strategies to unintended outcomes: the impact of change recipient sense making', *Organization Studies*, 26(11): 1573–1601

Bennis, W. G. 1969. *Organization development: its nature, origins and prospects.* Reading: Addison-Wesley

Berends, H., Debackere, K., Garud, R. and Weggeman, M. 2004. *Knowledge Integration by Thinking Along.* ECIS working paper

Berends, H. 2003. *Knowledge Sharing in Industrial Research.* Eindhoven: Eindhoven University Press

Bergman, R., Breen, S., Goker, M., Manago, M. and Wess, S. 1999. *Developing Industrial Case-Based Reasoning Applications – The INRECA Methodology.* Berlin: Springer Verlag

Berger, P. and Luckman, T. 1967. *The Social Construction of Reality.* New York, Garden City: Anchor

Bhaskar, R. 1986. *Scientific Realism and Human Emancipation.* London: Verso

Boer, A. 1989. *Toepasbaarheidsonderzoek IDEF-methoden.* Master thesis (in Dutch). Eindhoven: Eindhoven University of Technology

Brewerton, P. and Millward, L. 2001. *Organizational Research Methods.* London: Sage

Brown, S. L. and Eisenhardt, K. M. 1995. 'Product development: past research, present findings, and future directions', *Academy of Management Review*, 20(2): 343–78

Brunsson, N. 1985. *The Irrational Organization: Irrationality as a Basis for Organizational Action and Change.* Chichester: Wiley

Burgoyne, J. G. 1994. 'Stakeholder analysis', in C. Cassell and G. Symon (eds.) *Qualitative Methods in Organizational Research: a Practical Guide.* London: Sage, pp 187–207

Busby, J. S. 1999. 'The effectiveness of collective retrospection as a mechanism of organizational learning', *Journal of Applied Behavioral Science*, 35(1): 109–30

Casimir, H. 1983. *Haphazard Reality: Half a Century of Science.* New York: Harper & Row

Cassell, C. and Symon, G. 1994. *Qualitative Methods in Organizational Research: a Practical Guide.* London: Sage

The Certified Quality Manager Handbook 1999. Milwaukee: American Society for Quality

Checkland, P. and Scholes, J. 1990. *Soft Systems Methodology in Action.* Chicester: Wiley

Chell, E. 1998. 'Critical incident technique', in G. Symon and C. Cassell (eds.) *Qualitative Methods and Analysis in Organizational Research: a Practical Guide.* London: Sage, pp 51–72

Clark, P. A. 1972. *Action Research and Organizational Change.* London: Harper and Row

Chin, R. and Benne, K. D. 1976. 'General strategies for effecting change in human systems', in W. G. Bennis, K. D. Benne, R. Chin and K. E. Corey (eds.) *The Planning of Change.* New York: Holt, Rinehart and Winston

Cohen, M. D., March, J. G. and Olsen, J. P. 1972. 'A garbage can model of organizational choice', *Administrative Science Quarterly*, 17: 1–25

Cohen, S. G. and Bailey, D. E. 1997. 'What makes teams work: group effectiveness research from the shop floor to the executive suite', *Journal of Management*, 23(3): 239–90

Cook, T. D. and Campbell, D. T. 1979. *Quasi-experimentation.* Chicago: Rand McNally

Cooper, D. R. and Schindler, P. S. 2003. *Business Research Methods.* Boston: McGraw-Hill (eighth edition)

Cooper, H. M. 1998. *Synthesizing Research: a Guide for Literature Reviews.* Beverly Hills: Sage (third edition)

Cooper, H. M. and Hedges, L. V. 1993. *The Handbook of Research Synthesis.* New York: Russell Sage Foundation

Craig, E. (ed.) 1998. *Routledge Encyclopaedia of Philosophy.* London: Routledge

Cummings, T. G. and Worley, C. G. 2001. *Organizational Development and Change.* Mason: South-Western College Publishing (seventh edition)

Daft, R. L. and Lengel, R. H. 1986. 'Organizational information requirements, media richness and structural design', *Management Science* 32(5): 554–71

Davenport, T. H. and Prusak, L. 1998. *Working Knowledge.* Boston: Harvard Business School Press

De Groot, A. D. 1969. *Methodology: Foundations of Inference and Research in the Behavioral Sciences.* Den Haag: Mouton

DeSanctis, G. and Poole, M. S. 1994. 'Capturing the complexity in advanced technology use: adaptive structuration theory', *Organization Science* 5(2): 121–47

De Haan, E. 2004. *Learning with Colleagues.* Basingstoke: Palgrave Macmillan

Dewey, J. 1909. *How We Think.* London: Heath

Driehuis, M. 1997. *De Lerende Adviseur: een Onderzoek naar Intercollegiaal Consult in Organisatieadvisering.* PhD thesis (in Dutch). Eindhoven University of Technology

Eden, C. and Huxham, C. 1996. 'Action research for the study of organizations', In S. R. Clegg, C. Hardy and W. R. Nord (eds.) *Handbook of Organization Studies*, London: Sage, pp 526–42

Ericsson, K. A. and Simon, H. A. 1984. *Protocol Analysis: Verbal Reports as Data*. Cambridge: MIT Press

Evbuonwan, N. F. O., Sivaloganathan, S. and Jebb, A. 1996. 'A survey of design philosophies, models, methods and systems', *Proceedings Institute of Mechanical Engineers*, 210: 301–20

Faraj, S. and Sproull, L. 2000. 'Coordinating expertise in software development teams', *Management Science* 46(12): 1554–68

Flanagan, J. C. 1954. 'The critical incident technique', *Psychological Bulletin*, 51(2): 327–58

Forster, N. 1994. 'The analysis of company documentation', in C. Cassell and G. Symon (eds.) *Qualitative Methods in Organizational Research: a Practical Guide.* London: Sage, pp 147–66

French, W. L. and Bell, C. H. Jr 1999. *Organizational Development: Behavioral Science Interventions for Organizational Improvement.* Upper Saddle River: Prentice Hall (sixth edition)

Gass, S. I. and Harris, C. M. (eds.) 2001. *Encyclopaedia of Operations Research and Management Science.* Dordrecht: Kluwer Academic (second edition)

Gerards, S. J. T. 1998. *Interfacemanagement van het Zorgproces voor COPD-patiënten.* Master thesis (in Dutch). Eindhoven: Eindhoven University of Technology

Gherardi, S. and Nicolini, D. 2001. 'The sociological foundations of organizational learning', in M. Dierkes, A. B. Antal, J. Child and I. Nonaka (eds.) *Handbook of Organizational Learning and Knowledge.* Oxford: Oxford University Press, pp 35–60

Glaser, B. and Strauss, A. 1967. *The Discovery of Grounded Theory.* Chicago: Aldine

Glaser, B. 1978. *Theoretical Sensitivity.* Mill Valley: Sociology Press

Glaser, B. 1992. *Basics of Grounded Theory Analysis.* Mill Valley: Sociology Press

Goldman, A. I. 1999. *Knowledge in a Social World.* Oxford: Oxford University Press

Grant, R. M. 1996. 'Towards a knowledge-based theory of the firm', *Strategic Management Journal*, 17 (Winter Special Issue): 109–22

Guba, E. G. and Lincoln, Y. S. 1989. *Fourth Generation Evaluation.* Newbury Park: Sage Publications

Habermas, J. 1981. *Theorie des Kommunikativen Handelns.* Frankfurt: Suhrkamp

Hart, C. 2001. *Doing a Literature Search.* London: Sage Publications

Harzing, A. 2002. 'Are our referencing errors undermining our scholarship and credibility? The case of expatriate failure rates', *Journal of Organizational Behaviour*, 23(1): 127–48

Hatch, M. J. 1997. *Organization Theory.* Oxford: Oxford University Press

Heery, E. and M. Noon (eds.) 2001. *A Dictionary of Human Resource Management.* Oxford: Oxford University Press

Hicks, M. J. 1995. *Problem Solving in Business and Management: Hard, Soft and Creative Approaches.* London: Chapman and Hall

Hornby, P. and Symon, G. 1994. 'Tracer studies', in C. Cassell and G. Symon (eds.) *Qualitative Methods in Organizational Research.* London: Sage, pp 167–86

Huber, G. P. 1991. 'Organizational learning: the contributing processes and the literature', *Organization Science*, 2(1): 88–115

Ishikawa, K. 1990. *Introduction to Quality Control.* London: Chapman and Hall

Jankowicz, A. D. 2004. *Business Research Projects* (fourth edition). London: Thomson Learning

Johnson, G. I. and Briggs, P. 1994. 'Question-asking and verbal protocol techniques', in C. Cassell and G. Symon (eds.) *Qualitative Methods in Organizational Research*. London: Sage, pp 55–71

Johnson, P. and Duberley, J. 2000. *Understanding Management Research*. London: Sage

Kazdin, A. E. (ed.) 2000. *Encyclopaedia of Psychology*. Oxford: Oxford University Press

Kepner, C. H. and Tregoe, B. B. 1981. *The New Rational Manager*. Princeton: Kepner-Tregoe

Kempen, P. and Keizer, J. A. 2006 *Business Research, a Solution Oriented Approach*. London: Butterworth-Heinemann

King, N. 1994. 'The qualitative research interview', in C. Cassell and G. Symon (eds.) *Qualitative Methods in Organizational Research*. London: Sage, pp 14–36

Kotter, J. P. 1978. *Organizational Dynamics: Diagnosis and Interventions*. Amsterdam: Addison Wesley

Kubr, M (ed.) 1996. *Management Consulting, a Guide to the Profession*. Geneva: International Labour Office (third edition)

Kvale, S. 1996. *InterViews: an Introduction to Qualitative Research Interviewing*. London: Sage

Latour, B. 1987. *Science in Action*. Cambridge, MA: Harvard University Press

Lawson, H. and Appignanesi, L. (eds.) 1989. *Dismantling Truth: Reality in the Post-modern World*. London: Weidenfeld and Nicolson

Leake, D. B. 1996. *Case-Based Reasoning: Experiences, Lessons and Future Directions*. Menlo Park: American Association for Artificial Intelligence

Lewis-Beck, M. S., Bryman A. and Liao, T. F. (eds.) 2004. *Sage Encyclopaedia of Social Science Research Methods*. London: Sage

Light, R. J. and Pillemer, D. B. 1984. *Summing Up: the Science of Reviewing Research*. Cambridge: Harvard University Press

Lindblom, C. E. 1959. 'The science of muddling through', *Public Administration Review*, 79–88

March, J. G. and Simon, H. A. 1958. *Organizations*. New York: Wiley

Meeuwesen, S. 2005. *Knowledge Sharing within Rolls-Royce*. (Master Thesis.) Eindhoven: Eindhoven University of Technology

Miles, M. B. and Huberman, A. M. 1994. *Qualitative Data Analysis: an Expanded Sourcebook*. London: Sage (second edition)

Miyake, N. and Norman, D. A. 1979. 'To ask a question, one must know enough to know what is not known', *Journal of Verbal Learning and Verbal Behavior*, 18: 357–64

Mohr, L. B. 1982. *Explaining Organizational Behavior*. San Francisco: Jossey-Bass

Mohr, L. B. 1995. *Impact analysis for program evaluation*. Thousand Oaks: Sage

Monhemius, W. 1984. *Methoden van Toegepast Bedrijfskundig Onderzoek*. (Lecture notes) Eindhoven: Eindhoven University of Technology

Morgan, D. L. 1991. *Focus Groups as Qualitative Research*. Beverly Hills: Sage

Nason, J. and Golding, D. 1998. 'Approaching observation', in G. Symon and C. Cassell (eds.) *Qualitative Methods and Analysis in Organizational Research*. London: Sage, pp 234–49

Nederlands Normalisatie Instituut 1967. *NEN 3283*. (In Dutch.) Delft: NNI

Newell, A. and Simon, H. A. 1972. *Human Problem Solving*. Englewood Cliffs: Prentice-Hall

Newell, S., Robertson, M., Scarbrough, H. and Swan, J. 2002. *Managing Knowledge Work*. Houndmills: Palgrave

Nonaka, I. 1994. 'A dynamic theory of organizational knowledge creation', *Organization Science*, 5(1): 14–47

Numagami, T. 1998. 'The infeasibility of invariant laws in management studies: a reflective dialogue in defence of case studies', *Organization Science*, 9: 2–15

Nutt, P. C. 1984. 'Types of organizational decision processes', *Administrative Science Quarterly*, 29: 414–50

Pawson, R. 2002a. 'Evidence-based policy: the promise of 'realist synthesis'', *Evaluation*, 8(3): 340–58

Pawson, R. 2002b. 'Evidence and policy and naming and shaming', *Policy Studies*, 23(3/4): 211–30

Pelz, D. S. 1978. 'Some expanded perspectives on the use of social science in public policy', in M. Yinger and S. J. Cutler (eds.) *Major Social Issues: a Multidisciplinary View*. New York: Free Press 346–57

Pisano, G. 1994. 'Knowledge, integration and the locus of learning: an empirical analysis of process development', *Strategic Management Journal*, 15: 85–100

Polanyi, M. 1958. *Personal Knowledge*. London: Routledge and Kegan Paul

Popper, K. R. 1963. *Conjectures and Refutations*. London: Routledge and Kegan Paul

Quinn, J. B. 1980. *Strategies for Change: Logical Incrementalism*. Homewood: Irwin

Reason, P. and Bradbury, H. (eds.) 2001. *Handbook of Action Research: Participative Inquiry and Practice*. London: Sage

Reichenbach, H. 1938 *Experience and Prediction. An Analysis of the Foundations and the Structure of Knowledge*. Chicago: University of Chicago Press

Ryle, G. 1949. *The Concept of Mind*. Londen: Hutchinson

Salvendy, G. (ed.) 2001. *Handbook of Industrial Engineering*. Chichester: Wiley-Interscience (third edition)

Savransky, S. D. 2000. *Engineering of Creativity: Introduction to TRIZ Methodology of Inventive Problem Solving*. London: CRC-Press

Schaffer, R. H. 1997 *High Impact Consulting*. San Francisco: Jossey-Bass Publishers

Schein, E. H. 1969. *Process Consulting: its Role in Organizational Development*. Reading: Addison-Wesley

Schön, D. A. 1983. *The Reflective Practitioner*. London: Temple Smith

Searle, J. R. 1995. *The Construction of Social Reality*. London: Penguin Books

Silverman, D. 1970. *The Theory of Organizations*. London: Heineman

Simon, H. A. 1960. *The New Science of Management Decision*. New York: Harper and Row

Simon, H. A. 1996. *The Sciences of the Artificial*. Cambridge (MA): MIT Press (third edition; original edition 1969)

Simon, H. A. 1999. 'Problem solving', In R. A. Wilson and F. C. Keil (eds.) *The MIT Encyclopaedia of the Cognitive Sciences*. London: MIT Press, pp 674–6

Simonin, B. L. 1997. 'The importance of collaborative know-how: an empirical test of the learning organization', *Academy of Management Journal*, 40(5): 1150–74

Slevin, D. P. and Pinto, J. K. 1986. 'The project implementation profile: a new tool for project managers', *Project Management Journal*, 17(4): 57–70

Spradley, J. P. 1980. *Participant Observation*. New York: Holt

Steyaert, C. and Bouwen, R. 1994. 'Group methods of organizational analysis', in C. Cassell and G. Symon (eds.) *Qualitative Methods in Organizational Research*. London: Sage, pp 123–46

Strauss, A. 1987. *Qualitative Analysis for Social Scientists*. New York: Cambridge University Press

Strauss, A. and Corbin, J. 1998. *Basics of Qualitative Research*. Newbury Park: Sage Publications (second edition)

Susman, G. I. and Evered, R. D. 1978. 'An assessment of the scientific merits of action research', *Administrative Science Quarterly*, 23: 582–603

Swanborn, P. G. 1996. 'A common base for quality control criteria in quantitative and qualitative research', *Quality and Quantity*, 30: 19–35

Symon, G. 1998. 'Qualitative research diaries', in G. Symon and C. Cassell (eds.) *Qualitative Methods and Analysis in Organizational Research*. London: Sage, pp 94–117

Symon, G. and Cassell, C. 1998. *Qualitative Methods and Analysis in Organizational Research: a Practical Guide*. London: Sage

Tichy, N. M. 1983 *Managing Strategic Change: Technical, Political and Cultural Dynamics*. Chichester: Wiley International

Tranfield, D., Denyer, D. and Smart, P. 2003. 'Towards a methodology for developing evidence-informed management knowledge by means of systematic review', *British Journal of Management*, 14: 207–22

Tsoukas, H. and Knudsen, C. (eds.) 2003. *The Oxford Handbook of Organization Theory*. Oxford: Oxford University Press

Tushman, M. L. 1978. 'Technical communication in R&D laboratories: the impact of project work characteristics', *Academy of Management Journal*. 21(4): 624–45

Tushman M. L. and Nadler, D. A. 1978. 'Information processing as an integrating concept in organizational design', *Academy of Management Review*, 3(3): 613–23

Van Aken, J. E. 2002. *Strategievorming en Organisatiestructurering*. (In Dutch) Deventer: Kluwer (second edition)

Van Aken, J. E. 2004. 'Management research based on the paradigm of the design sciences: the quest for tested and grounded technological rules', *Journal of Management Studies*, 41(2): 219–46

Van Aken, J. E. 2005a. 'Management research as a design science: articulating the research products of mode 2 knowledge production', *British Journal of Management*, 16: 19–39

Van Aken, J. E. 2005b. 'Valid knowledge for the professional design of large and complex design processes', *Design Studies*, 26: 379–404

Van der Wiel, M. W. J., Szegedi, K. H. P. and Weggeman, M. C. D. P. 2004. 'Professional learning: deliberate attempts at developing expertise', in H. P. A. Boshuizen, R. Bromme and H. Gruber (eds.) *Professional Learning*. Dordrecht: Kluwer Academic, pp 181–206

Van de Ven, A. H. and Poole, M. S. 1995. 'Explaining development and change in organizations', *Academy of Management Review*, 20(3): 510–40

Van de Ven, A. H., Polley, D. E. and Garud, R. 1999. *The Innovation Journey*. Oxford: Oxford University Press

Van Dijk, J., De Goede, M., Hart, H. and Teunissen, J. 1991. *Onderzoeken & Veranderen: Methoden van Praktijkonderzoek*. Houten: Stenfert Kroese

Van Maanen, J. 1988. *Tales of the Field: on Writing Ethnography*. Chicago: University of Chicago Press

Van Meurs, C. 1997. *Procesbeheersing in de Logistiek*. Master thesis (in Dutch). Eindhoven University of Technology

Van Strien, P. J. 1997. 'Towards a methodology of psychological practice', *Theory and Psychology*, 7(5): 683–700

Van Vuuren, W. 1993. *SAFER: Near Miss Rapportage bij Hoogovens IJmuiden*. (Master Thesis) Eindhoven: Eindhoven University of Technology

Verschuren, P. and Doorewaard, H. 1999. *Designing a Research Project*. Utrecht: Lemma

Von Zedtwitz, M. 2002. 'Organizational learning through post-project reviews in R&D', *R&D Management*, 32(3): 255–68

Waddington, D. 1994. 'Participant observation', in C. Cassell and G. Symon (eds.) *Qualitative Methods in Organizational Research*. London: Sage, pp 107–22

Walsh, J. P. 1995. 'Managerial and organizational cognition: notes from a trip down memory lane', *Organization Science* 6(3): 280–321

Warner, M. (ed.) 1996. *International Encyclopaedia of Business and Management*. London: Routledge

Watson, I. 1997. *Applying Case-Based Reasoning: Techniques for Enterprise Systems*, San Francisco: Morgan Kaufman Publishers

Weick K. E. 1993. 'Organizational redesign as improvisation', in G. P. Huber and W. H. Glick (eds.) *Organizational Change and Redesign: Ideas and Insights for Improving Performance*, New York: Oxford University Press, pp 346–82

Weick, K. E. 1995. *Sensemaking in Organizations*. London: Sage Publications

Wenger, E. 1998. *Communities-of-Practice*. Cambridge: Cambridge University Press

Whitley, R. 1984. *The Intellectual and Social Organization of the Sciences*. Oxford: Clarendon Press

Wickham, P. A. 1999 *Management Consulting*. London: Financial Times Management

Witte, E. 1972. 'Field research on complex decision-making processes – the phase theorem', *International Studies in Management and Organization*, 2: 156–82

Worren, N., Moore, K and Elliott, R. 2002. 'When theories become tools: toward a framework for pragmatic validity', *Human Relations* 55(10): 1227–50

Yin, R. K. 1994. *Case Study Research: Design and Methods*. Thousand Oaks: Sage Publications (second edition)

Index

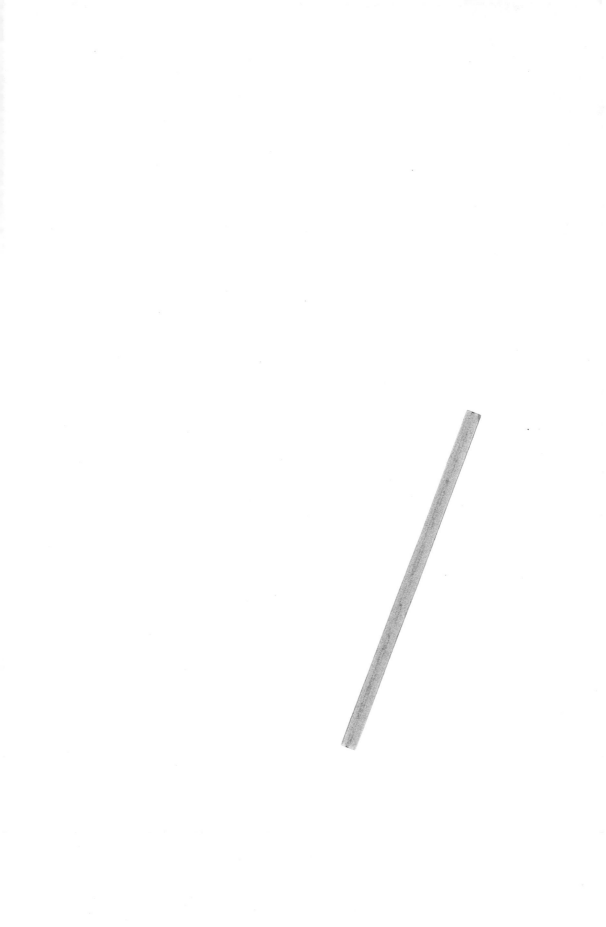